CHARLESTON UNDER SIEGE

THE IMPREGNABLE CITY

D1738456

DOUGLAS W. BOSTICK

Charleston   London

History
PRESS

Published by The History Press
Charleston, SC 29403
www.historypress.net

Copyright © 2010 by Douglas W. Bostick
All rights reserved

Cover image: Currier and Ives print of the ill-fated ironclad attack on Fort Sumter,
April 7, 1863. *Courtesy of the Library of Congress.*

First published 2010

Manufactured in the United States

ISBN 978.1.59629.757.9

Library of Congress Cataloging-in-Publication Data

Bostick, Douglas W.
Charleston under siege : the impregnable city / Douglas W. Bostick.
p. cm.
Includes bibliographical references and index.
ISBN 978-1-59629-757-9
1. Charleston (S.C.)--History--Civil War, 1861-1865. 2. Charleston (S.C.)--History--Siege,
1863. I. Title.
E470.65.B73 2010
975.7'91503--dc22
2010044803

This book is dedicated to my son, Taylor. Though not always wanting to admit it to his dad, he loves the many stories of the history of the South Carolina Lowcountry. He encourages me in my pursuit as a writer. Just when I take what I do too seriously, he makes me laugh and keeps me focused on my most important job—being a father.

Contents

Acknowledgements   7

1. "Great Terror Prevailing"   9
2. "So Unworthy"   19
3. "Panic and Disaster Were Imminent"   26
4. "Completely at My Mercy"   39
5. "The Turrets Are Coming"   57
6. "Men Fell by the Scores"   68
7. "A Swamp Angel Will Preach"   85
8. "Hell Can't Be Worse"   93
9. "Must Be Held to the Bitter End"   98
10. "Cigar Steamer for Carrying Spar Torpedoes"   107
11. "Wonderful Fish-Shaped Boat"   113
12. "Its Inhumane Threat"   122
13. "A Terrible, Heart-Breaking, Awful Night"   132

Bibliography   149
Index   153
About the Author   159

ACKNOWLEDGEMENTS

The story of the Siege of Charleston is often lost in the shadow of the drama of the "first shot" on April 12, 1861, that started the Civil War. The 1989 movie *Glory* showcased the July 18, 1863 attack on Battery Wagner. The world watched as the *H.L. Hunley* was located and recovered from Charleston Harbor, reminding us all of the first successful attack on an enemy warship by a submarine. These stories, however, are only pieces of the greater story—the longest siege of the Civil War.

I am indebted to writers and historians who preceded me in preserving the great tales of the defense of Charleston. Skipper Keith has been an incredible resource to many writers, myself included. Though he completed a successful career with the South Carolina Department of Natural Resources, I know of no one more knowledgeable about the Civil War in the South Carolina Lowcountry. Rick Hatcher, historian at Fort Sumter National Monument, has always graciously fielded my questions and offered his critique.

I am also indebted to my family for their understanding, encouragement and support. They tolerate many hours that I am locked away in my office, staring at my computer monitor, trying to figure out the perfect wording. Just when I think they are not paying attention to my stories of local history, they respond with a nugget during an after-dinner game of Bostick family trivia.

Most of all, I am overwhelmed in my admiration for the men, Confederate and Union, who answered the call of their countries. Their bravery and selflessness are awe inspiring.

1

"Great Terror Prevailing"

It was almost 4:30 p.m. on April 14, 1861, when, after withstanding an intense bombardment, Major Robert Anderson and his beleaguered garrison marched out of Fort Sumter to the tune of "Yankee Doodle," followed by "Hail to the Chief," thus ending the first chapter of a four-year-long civil war. Later that evening in Charleston, South Carolina governor Francis Pickens made a speech from the balcony of the Charleston Hotel in which he declared:

> We have defeated their twenty millions. We have humbled the flag of the United States before the Palmetto and Confederate, and so long as I have the honor to preside as your chief magistrate, so help me God, there is no power on earth shall ever lower from that fortress those flags, unless they be lowered and trailed in a sea of blood. I can here say to you it is the first time in the history of this country that the stars and stripes have been humbled. That flag has never before been lowered before any nation on this earth. But today it has been humbled and humbled before the glorious little State of South Carolina.

On April 15, 1861, U.S. president Abraham Lincoln issued a proclamation calling for seventy-five thousand troops "to re-possess the forts, places, and property which have been seized from the Union." He also called for both houses of Congress to convene on July 4 to "consider and determine, such measures, as, in their wisdom, the public safety, and interest may seem to demand."

Illustration of the firing on Fort Sumter, April 12, 1861, published in *Harper's Weekly*. *Author's collection*.

Harper's Weekly engraving of the Confederate flag now flying over Fort Sumter, April 15, 1861, after the evacuation of the Federal garrison. *Author's collection*.

On April 19, 1861, Lincoln ordered the blockade of all Southern ports from South Carolina to Texas. The next day, the Gosport Navy Yard at Norfolk was captured by the Confederacy. William Mahone, president of the Norfolk and Petersburg Railroad, tricked the Union troops at Gosport into evacuation. He bluffed the Union command by running a passenger train in and out of Norfolk, repeatedly blowing the whistle, leaving the Northerners with the impression that a large Confederate force was assembling for an attack. The Union troops withdrew to Fort Monroe at Hampton Roads, and the Confederacy seized the Gosport Navy Yard, the largest shipyard and logistical base of the U.S. Navy. At the navy yard, the Confederates also seized more than $8 million in property, including three thousand pieces of ordnance, among them Dahlgren guns, the navy's latest and most modern naval weapon.

Charleston was a point of immediate attention for the Union ships moving to form the blockade. Not only was it the "cradle of secession," but also its proximity to Bermuda (780 miles) and Nassau (500 miles) made the South Carolina port a key connection for blockade runners. Once goods reached Charleston, its strategic railroad connections allowed vital supplies to be distributed throughout the South. The goal of the blockade, quite simply, was to prevent cotton from leaving the port and finished goods, food and military supplies from entering the port, thus choking off Charleston and the Confederacy.

On May 11, 1861, the steam frigate USS *Niagara* was the first ship to arrive at the mouth of Charleston Harbor to initiate the blockade. The warship was one of the fastest ships in the U.S. Navy and was heavily armed with nine guns. However, with a deep draft of twenty-four feet, the blockading frigate could only cover the main channel, leaving three other shallower harbor entrances open.

The *Niagara* had visited Charleston previously when a slave trader, the *Echo*, was seized while illegally transporting captured Africans. The captain and crew of the *Echo* were placed on trial for piracy and murder. The Africans were held in protective custody, first at Castle Pinckney and later at the unfinished Fort Sumter. Custody of the Africans was ultimately transferred to the Society for the Colonization of Free People of Color. On September 21, 1858, the USS *Niagara* picked up the surviving 271 Africans and transported them to Monrovia, Liberia, for resettlement.

In its second day on patrol, the *Niagara* could only watch as the *A and A*, a bark from Belfast, steamed past utilizing one of the other channels, marking the event as the first ship to run the blockade. Later on May 12, another first occurred when the *Niagara* seized the *General Parkhill*, a British ship from Liverpool, the first blockade runner captured by the Union navy.

Charleston resident Emma Holmes wrote in her diary, "Old Abe has at last fulfilled his threats of blockading us by sending us the *Niagara* here."

Shortly, the USS *Seminole*, USS *Wabash*, USS *Vandalia* and the revenue cutter USS *Harriet Lane* arrived at Charleston, joining the *Niagara* on patrol. When the *Wabash* arrived, it collided with the *Seminole*, mistaking the *Seminole* for a blockade runner. Even with these ships' arrival, the blockade was still largely ineffective as the ships patrolled up and down the Southern Atlantic coast. Additionally, they were constantly steaming to Hampton Roads, Virginia, or Pensacola, Florida, to refuel with coal. This often left only one ship stationed at Charleston. Captain Samuel Mercer of the *Wabash*, in a report to Washington, stated, "You know as well as I do that to blockade this port with this ship alone is next door to an impossibility."

On September 28, Commander Samuel Phillips Lee aboard the *Vandalia* came close to sparking an international incident. He spotted a vessel thought to be a blockade runner quickly moving to enter Charleston Harbor. Lee ordered his crew to quarters and fired a warning shot ahead of the vessel. He then sent a boarding party to inspect the ship. On arrival, the boarding party realized they had fired on the HMS *Steady*, a British gunboat dispatched to Charleston to communicate with the British consul there.

Blockade running became big business in Charleston. John Fraser & Company in Charleston was a leading firm in providing the Confederacy with war supplies. Though many ships successfully ran the Union blockade, food and personal goods were becoming scarcer, and prices for items that did reach Charleston were high. One Charleston merchant observed, "The blockade is still carried on and every article of consumption particularly in the way of groceries…[is] getting very high."

In the first six weeks after the surrender of Fort Sumter, more than thirty thousand bales of cotton shipped out of Charleston. Between June and December 1861, more than 150 vessels successfully arrived at Charleston using the interior waterways rather than the main shipping channel.

The Confederacy also worked with citizen privateers by issuing them a "Letter of Marque," granting them a commission to seize enemy shipping off the Southern coast. One privateer, the *Jefferson Davis*, captured nine merchant vessels during the summer of 1861.

The Southern blockade, with much coastline to cover, continued to be ineffective, and on June 27, 1861, Secretary of the Navy Gideon Welles appointed the "Commission of Conference," nicknamed by many the

"Blockade Strategy Board." The committee members were Professor Alexander Bache, superintendent of the U.S. Coast Survey; John G. Barnard, chief engineer of the U.S. Army; navy captain Charles H. Davis; and navy captain Samuel Francis Du Pont, chairman of the commission. The commission, charged with the responsibility to make recommendations for the blockade strategy, met frequently from July to September at the Smithsonian Institution in Washington.

In a report on July 13, 1861, the commission recommended that a port of operations be established to support the South Atlantic blockade. Their three choices for consideration were Bull's Bay, north of Charleston, and St. Helena Sound and Port Royal Sound, south of Charleston. The choice of St. Helena or Port Royal could also support Federal operations against Savannah. Port Royal, considered to be the finest natural deep-water harbor south of the Chesapeake Bay, was ultimately selected. They calculated that a force of six thousand men would be needed to capture Hilton Head, Parry's Island (now Parris Island) and Phillip's Island. Further, they estimated that ten to twelve thousand troops would be required to hold that position on the South Carolina coast.

On August 27, U.S. flag officer Silas Horton Stringham led an expedition to Hatteras Inlet and forced the surrender of the Confederate forts there. Welles gave Du Pont the command of the South Atlantic Blockading Squadron, which was responsible for the Atlantic coast from the North Carolina–South Carolina border to Key West. Welles also instructed Du Pont to organize his own expedition south.

After the fall of Fort Sumter, Brigadier General P.G.T. Beauregard began enhancing the defenses on the South Carolina coast. Governor Pickens, however, asked that two forts be constructed at the entrance to the Port Royal Harbor: Fort Walker on Hilton Head and Fort Beauregard at Bay Point. On May 27, 1861, Beauregard departed South Carolina for Virginia, and Captain Francis D. Lee, South Carolina Army Engineers, was tasked with building the two new forts.

Work on Forts Walker and Beauregard began in July 1861, utilizing slave labor from local plantations. Fort Walker was constructed with twelve guns trained on the harbor and ten guns installed on the rear and right flank to address any land attack. Fort Beauregard had thirteen guns trained on the harbor and six mounted to defend against a ground attack.

By August, Union brigadier general Thomas W. Sherman was ordered by the secretary of war to start recruiting an army in the New England states for an attack on the Southern coast. Flag Officer Du Pont was assigned

Union brigadier general Thomas Sherman.
Courtesy of the Library of Congress.

the responsibility for the naval expedition to coordinate with Sherman. The army assembled 12,653 troops and thirty-six transports at Annapolis, Maryland, while Du Pont used New York to organize fifteen warships with a total of 148 guns. Sherman and Du Pont rendezvoused at Hampton Roads, Virginia.

On October 28, the coal and ammunition ships, escorted by the USS *Vandalia* and the USS *Gem of the Sea*, departed Hampton Roads. The next day, the warships and troop transports departed en route to Port Royal, South Carolina. The captain of each ship was provided with sealed orders with their destination, only to be opened at sea. Despite the efforts to keep the mission secret, the *New York Times* published a front-page article entitled "The Great Naval Expedition," providing the Confederacy with the details and destination of the campaign.

Once the fleet entered South Carolina waters, it encountered a large storm. Several ships had to return to Hampton Roads for repairs. The USS *Isaac P. Smith* had to dump its guns to stay afloat. Three ships—the USS *Union*, the USS *Peerless* and the USS *Osceola*, carrying food, supplies and ammunition—were lost.

The first of the Federal fleet arrived at Port Royal by November 3. By November 7, most of the Federal ships surviving the sea journey were all in place. On November 4, the USS *Vixen*, a coast survey ship, was escorted by the warships USS *Ottawa*, USS *Seneca*, USS *Pembina* and USS *Penguin* to conduct sounding for the charts for Port Royal Sound. The CSS *Savannah*, CSS *Resolute*, CSS *Lady Davis* and CSS *Sampson* moved in to confront the Union ships, but the firepower of the heavily armed enemy chased them off.

The next day, six Union warships entered the harbor to draw fire from the forts to measure their strength and number of guns. The two Confederate forts opened fire, and the four Confederate gunboats again challenged the Union ships but were once again chased off.

Though the U.S. Navy was ready to attack, the army was unprepared. The landing ships were lost in the storm at sea, as was much of their ammunition. Sherman was waiting for the arrival of the USS *Ocean Express*, transporting additional ammunition and heavy ordnance.

An 1861 engraving of flag officer Samuel F. Du Pont, published in *Harper's Weekly. Author's Collection.*

Du Pont would not agree to delay and ordered an attack by his warships for November 5. However, as the USS *Wabash* moved into the sound, it ran aground on Fishing Rip Shoal. The decision was made to delay the attack one day. The next day, though, was stormy, and the attack was set back one more day.

Finally, on November 7, the weather was favorable, and the Federal ships formed in two columns. The main column included the flagship *Wabash*, followed by the *Susquehanna, Mohican, Seminole, Pawnee, Unadilla, Ottawa, Pembina* and *Isaac P. Smith* towing the *Vandalia*. The flanking column included the *Bienville, Seneca, Penguin, Curlew* and *Augusta*. The warships *R.B. Forbes, Mercury* and *Penguin* were held back to protect the troop transports.

The Confederates at Fort Walker fired the first shot at the approaching column of gunboats at 9:26 a.m. Quickly, the guns facing the harbor at both forts were engaged. The Union fleet executed its plan of maneuvering in a column, turning left and reengaging. The Confederate artillery was

Union attack on Port Royal, November 7, 1861. *Author's collection.*

ineffective against the moving warships. After the first turn, some Union ships' captains made independent decisions to pull out of column seeking particular firing positions. Commander Sylanus Godon aboard the *Mohican* moved to fire on a Confederate battery. The three ships behind the *Mohican*, now confused, also broke formation. Only the *Wabash* and *Susquehanna* followed the plan, making three passes.

The forts and Union ships exchanged fire until just past noon. The *Pocahontas*, delayed in its arrival to Port Royal, joined in the attack on Fort Walker. Commander Percival Drayton, commander of the Union warship *Pocahontas*, faced his brother, Confederate general Thomas Drayton, directing the action at Fort Walker.

Confederate colonel John A. Wagener, First Artillery, South Carolina Militia, wrote of the fight at Fort Walker:

> *The sailing vessels of our opponents were towed by steamers, and thus could maneuver on the broad expanse of Port Royal with the accuracy of well trained battalions. No sooner did we obtain his range than it would be changed…while the deep water permitted him to choose his own position, and fire shot after shot.*

By 12:30 p.m., Fort Walker had only three guns still operational. By 2:00 p.m., these guns were out of powder and the troops abandoned the fort. Seeing the departure of the Confederate troops, Union commander G.W. Rodgers led a boat crew to shore and, finding Fort Walker completely abandoned, raised the U.S. flag over the fort.

Fort Beauregard had not suffered as much damage and could still return fire. Confederate colonel R.G.M. Dunovant, realizing that Fort Walker was now abandoned, ordered his men to quietly withdraw. The Union fleet only realized it was evacuated when there was no return fire.

The Confederates suffered eleven men killed, forty-seven wounded and four missing in action. The Union fleet only had eight men killed and twenty-three wounded. While the causalities were small, the victory provided the Union army and navy what they badly needed—a Southern base of operations.

The Battle of Port Royal was the first major Union victory in the war. It bolstered spirits in the North and caused much concern in South Carolina. One resident in Charleston wrote, "There is great terror prevailing here…I regard the city in hourly peril. I believe it could be taken in hours." Though

Federal brigade taking possession of Beaufort, December 5, 1861. *Author's collection.*

he was no longer commanding troops in South Carolina, some members of the South Carolina state convention criticized Beauregard for his plans to defend the coast, even though the plans for the defense of Port Royal were developed by Governor Pickens.

Charlestonian Emma Holmes wrote of the Confederate defeat at Port Royal in her diary:

> [General Ripley] *had scarcely arrived at Hardeeville, when courier after courier galloped panting in, almost fainting from exhaustion, to say that our men had retreated. At first it was not believed, but when successive ones arrived with the same astounding news, he asked, "of course in order," but was horrified by the answer, "No, in great disorder." Gen Drayton alas fully proved his utter incompetency for his high position, but I sincerely pity him. To have been raised from an honorable position as a citizen respected by all to a distinguished military one from which he has gained nothing but contempt. However, I think the battle of Port Royal has been a great service to us, by arousing everyone from their dangerous security to the utmost vigilance & activity. The Beaufort planters will no doubt suffer greatly, but they deserve it in a great measure, for they would not remove their negroes and valuables in time, as they were long ago warned to do; as to the Yankees, the little cotton & provisions they have obtained won't pay half the expense of the expedition, and I have not the slightest doubt their dreadful treatment of the negroes, at least the men, will assuredly strengthen our "peculiar institution" by teaching them who are their true friends.*

A report of the affair by General Roswell Ripley's staff asserted:

> *The troops of the fort* [Fort Walker] *fought with great courage and determination. At Bay Point* [Fort Beauregard] *the order to retreat was felt to be judicious, but the soldiers were anxious to remain and battle it out to the last.*

More than half of the Union navy's ammunition was expended in the Battle of Port Royal. It would be three weeks before additional supplies would arrive. Du Pont constructed extensive facilities at Port Royal to maintain his fleet, including supply depots for coal and provisions and ship repair facilities.

2

"So Unworthy"

The Confederate authorities in Richmond organized the Department of South Carolina, Georgia and East Florida and appointed General Robert E. Lee as commander. Lee arrived in Charleston by train on November 6. Knowing of the large Federal expedition off the coast of Port Royal, he immediately traveled south the next morning.

However, as Lee was en route, the Federal fleet attacked and captured the two Confederate forts. Lee later reported to Richmond the aftermath of the battle:

> On the evening of the 7th, on my way to the entrance of Port Royal Harbor, I met General Ripley…He reported that the enemy's fleet had passed the batteries and entered the harbor….Nothing could then be done but to make arrangements to withdraw the troops…General Drayton reports he has but 955 men with him, and no field battery…Colonel Dunovant's regiment is in as destitute a condition as General Drayton's command, as they were obliged to leave everything behind, and number between 600 and 700 men.

General Roswell Ripley wired the Confederate secretary of war, Judah P. Benjamin, requesting authority to declare martial law. Since Lee had already arrived in South Carolina, Benjamin responded that the decision was Lee's to make. With Union general Thomas Sherman making no immediate moves outside of Hilton Head, Lee did not institute martial law.

Lee's task to defend Charleston and Savannah was large, given the limited resources in place. In one of his first reports to Benjamin, Lee observed:

The enemy, having complete possession of the water and inland navigation, commands all the islands on this coast, and threatens both Savannah and Charleston, and can come in his boats within 4 miles of this place…I fear there are but few State troops ready for the field. The garrisons of the forts at Charleston and Savannah and on the coast cannot be removed from the batteries while ignorant of the designs of the enemy. I am endeavoring to bring into the field such light batteries as can be prepared.

While Lee was determining how to defend South Carolina and Georgia, the Union navy was exploring new strategies to blockade Savannah and Charleston, given that it did not have a sufficient number of warships to do the job. The Blockade Strategy Board advocated blockading the shipping channels with a "stone fleet"—sunken schooners filled with granite. Given the shallow depths in the harbors, the stone fleet could effectively prevent deep-draft vessels from entering or exiting the harbor.

In mid-October 1861, Federal secretary of the navy Gideon Welles ordered the purchase of twenty-five obsolete vessels at least 250 tons in size. The first ships were to be sent to Savannah and a second group sent to Charleston. The ships were purchased at an average price of $15,000 each, loaded with stone. Each ship had a five-inch knockout plug installed in the hull that could be removed to sink it once placed in the harbor channel. In a ruse played on any observers, the ships were painted with a white horizontal stripe with black squares at regular intervals. At a distance, these black squares would appear to be gun ports, leading an observer to the conclusion that these ships were warships.

On November 17, Secretary Welles wrote to Du Pont about Charleston:

It is believed that a new channel now exists bearing about due east from the light [on Morris Island]. *If this can be thoroughly closed, and only a few vessels sunk in the intricate channel of Sullivan's Island, Charleston as a harbor will no longer exist.*

On November 20, 1861, twenty-five schooners departed New Bedford, Massachusetts, bound for Savannah. When the ships arrived on December 3, Confederate forces panicked at the sight of so many "warships" appearing off the coast. As a defense, they sank their own vessels in the shipping channel to prevent the Union ships' approach. With the Confederate defense blocking the channel for them, the Union stone fleet was redirected to Charleston.

Sinking of the "stone fleet" in Charleston Harbor, December 1861. *Author's collection.*

Union captain Charles Henry Davis, Du Pont's chief of staff, was assigned the responsibility of sinking the ships at Charleston. Davis was a curious choice for the task given that he and Charles Boutelle of the Coast Survey did not believe that the sunken ships would effectively block the harbor. Many years earlier, Davis had been assigned to survey Charleston and Savannah Harbors to plan navigational improvements. In a letter to his family dated December 2, Davis stated:

> *The pet idea of Mr. Fox* [assistant secretary of the navy] *has been to stop up some of the southern harbors…I had always a special disgust for this business…I always considered this mode of interrupting commerce as liable to great objections and of doubtful success.*

The stone fleet arrived off Charleston Harbor on December 17. Initial ships were sunk on the east and west sides of the main harbor channel to serve as boundaries. The other ships were sunk in a checkerboard pattern across the channel. On December 25 and 26, 1861, thirteen additional

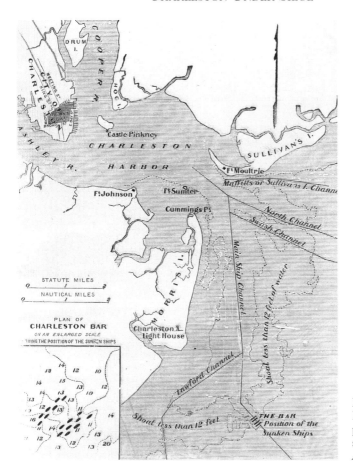

Map of Charleston Harbor noting the placement of the stone fleet barricade. *Author's collection.*

ships arrived in Charleston and were sunk across Maffit's Channel at the harbor entrance.

The *New York Times* declared the sunken stone fleet to be "unconquerable obstacles." A reporter from the *New York Herald* was present when the stone fleet was sunk. In his report, he offered, "One feels that at least one cursed rathole has been closed and one avenue of supplies cut off by the hulks."

The *Charleston Mercury*, predictably, had a different view of the stone fleet, offering:

> *On the occurrence of the first heavy northeaster, after the sinking of the wrecks, the force of the wind, the heave of the sea and the action of the quick-sands, will according to all previous experiences dissipate the Yankee obstruction.*

In a report to Secretary of War Benjamin, Lee reflected his surprise and disdain for the decision to block the harbor with the stone fleet, stating:

> *This achievement, so unworthy of any nation, is the abortive expression of malice and revenge of a people which it wishes to perpetuate by rendering more memorable a day hateful in their calendar. It is also indicative of their despair of ever capturing a city they design to ruin.*

His witness to the placement of the stone fleet forever changed Lee's view of the conduct of the war. He assumed that the war would be fought by gentlemen focusing on military targets. Instead, blockading the harbor would affect the many women, children and unarmed citizens in Charleston.

Lee was not the only person to object to the sinking of the stone fleet. The newspapers in Europe expressed their shock at the action taken. The *London Times* declared, "Among the crimes which have disgraced the history of mankind it would be difficult to find one more atrocious than this." U.S. secretary of state William Seward placated the European nations by suggesting it was "all a mistake."

Davis and Boutelle were correct in their assessment of the stone fleet. The strategy did not work. By the spring of 1862, the current had scoured the channel twenty-one feet deep at low tide, deeper than before the sinking of the ships.

Lee established his headquarters at Coosawatchie, South Carolina, and spent much of his time traveling the coast between Charleston and Savannah inspecting the coastal fortifications. He knew that the Union resources in ships, troops and provisions at Port Royal far outweighed anything at his disposal. In writing to Governor Pickens, Lee pointed out that the force of the Union army and navy "can be thrown with great celerity against any point, and far outnumber any force we can bring against it in the field."

Understanding his limitations, Lee devised a strategy of positioning troops and resources along the Charleston and Savannah Railroad lines where they could be quickly relocated to meet an attack.

On December 11, 1861, Lee was traveling with his staff from Coosawhatchie to Charleston. As they were crossing the Ashley River into Charleston, they could see a fire burning in the city. Mrs. C.E. Chicheshee, at Castle Pinckney in the harbor, wrote of the fire:

> *It commenced about 8 o'clock in the night…there was a slight wind blowing from the north-east, it spread slowly, as the tide rose, the wind increased and*

the fire spread rapidly…it soon passed beyond the control of the firemen who had only the old hand engines and wells and cisterns to aid them… Furniture and bedding was carried out into the wide streets, squares and vacant lots, little children and sick ones placed on the bedding, which soon took fire from the sparks falling all around, and the children had to be rescued, some by a stranger…At the Castle, the fire was soon observed by the sentinels, and the entire garrison watched it anxiously…my husband made a detail of as many men as the post boat could possibly carry and sent them over to the city to render what assistance they could…I was lying in bed suffering from a most excruciating headache…my colored maid, the man cook and the waiting man were in the next room where they could see and note the progress of the fire…truly it was a fearful night.

Not appreciating the size of the fire, Lee and his staff continued to the Mills House Hotel for dinner. As they received news of the destruction of the fire, Lee viewed the city from the hotel's rooftop and decided to evacuate the hotel to meet elsewhere in the city.

The fire burned more than 540 acres in the city, destroying or damaging almost six hundred homes, businesses, public buildings and churches. Estimates of the property losses were as high as $8 million. Charlestonian Emma Holmes, in her diary, wrote of the fire, "Hour after hour of anxiety passed, while flames raged more fiercely and the heavens illuminated as if it were an aurora borealis—it was terrifically beautiful."

On December 16, Lee reported to Benjamin on the defenses around Charleston:

The island defenses around the city, commencing on the coast side of James Island, extending to Wappoo Creek, thence to Ashley River, across the neck between Ashley and Cooper, and from the branch through Christ Church Parish to the sound, are in good state of progress, and will now give steadiness and security to our troops in any advance of the enemy from any of those quarters, and afford time to move troops to meet them. The works have been mostly constructed by labor furnished by the planters. I hope they will be complete this week. The batteries in the harbor are in good condition, and if properly served should arrest the approach by the channel. Wappoo Creek is also provided with batteries in addition to those previously constructed at the mouth of the Stono, which should stop vessels by that direction. They form part of the land defense and points of support where they touch the creek.

"So Unworthy"

In early January 1862, the Sovereign Convention of the State of South Carolina met in Charleston. On January 8, the convention declared:

> *The sense of the people of South Carolina, assembled in convention, that Charleston should be defended at any cost of life or property, and that, in their deliberate judgment, they would prefer a repulse of the enemy with the entire city in ruins, to an evacuation or surrender on any terms whatever.*

With the Union forces remaining quiet in Hilton Head in January 1862, Lee could only ponder their next target. On January 8, 1862, in a report to Adjutant General Cooper, Lee summarized his speculations about the enemy:

> *I have thought his purpose would be to seize upon the Charleston and Savannah Railroad near the head of Broad River, sever the line of communication between those cities with one of his columns of land troops, and with his other two and his fleet by water envelope alternately each of those cities. This would be a difficult combination for us successfully to resist.*

Though no advances had yet been made on Charleston, tensions in the city were high. One Charlestonian confided in his diary, "There has not been any year of our life that has passed, that has been fraught with so many events which will ever be remembered and which should indelibly imprint on our minds the instability and uncertainty of all our hopes and expectations." Another Charleston diarist wrote, "The fiercest wrath and bitterest indignation are directed towards Charleston, by 'our dearly beloved brethren of the North.' They say 'the rebellion commenced where Charleston is, and shall end, where Charleston was.'"

Lee was in Savannah on March 2, 1862, when he received a telegram from Jefferson Davis instructing him to report to Richmond. Brigadier General John C. Pemberton, serving in Lee's command, was promoted to major general and assigned to replace Lee.

3

"Panic and Disaster Were Imminent"

Union brigadier general Thomas W. Sherman requested Captain Quincy A. Gillmore, his chief engineer, to formulate several options for the capture of Charleston. Gillmore, a talented engineer, proposed two options. The first plan focused on Fort Sumter as the key to Charleston. Troops would make amphibious landings on Sullivan's and Morris Islands to create a crossfire on Fort Sumter. Once Fort Sumter capitulated, the Union fleet would sail into the inner harbor and force the surrender of the city. The second option used James Island as the gateway to Charleston. Moving across the island after a landing on the shoreline, Union siege batteries could be placed on the island's northern shore. This maneuver would not only leave the harbor forts vulnerable but would also allow the Union army to fire directly into Charleston, forcing its sure surrender.

In March 1862, Sherman was replaced by Major General David Hunter, who had served as commander of the Western Department since November 1861. While the army changed command, Flag Officer Du Pont retained command of the South Atlantic Blockading Squadron.

On March 27, 1862, Pemberton ordered Ripley to withdraw a battery from Coles Island at the mouth of the Stono River. Governor Pickens wired Lee in Richmond questioning this decision and Pemberton's earlier decision to remove the heavy guns at Georgetown, north of Charleston. Lee politely responded to the governor that as commander in South Carolina, Pemberton was in the best position to make that call. However, in a letter to Pemberton, Lee cautioned:

"Panic and Disaster Were Imminent"

It is respectively submitted to your judgment whether in order to preserve harmony between the State and Confederate authorities, it would not be better to notify the Governor whenever you determined to abandon any position of your line of defenses.

Pickens was distrustful of Pemberton, a Pennsylvanian by birth. The news of the abandonment of Coles Island was not well received in Charleston. One Charleston diarist wrote:

Our troops have evacuated Coles Island and Battery Island at the mouth of the Stono River. This is another example of weakness and vacillation in our military leaders; one erects a fortification at enormous expense and another destroys it. Our waggon has a team hitched to each end and they draw in opposite directions—what will become of the waggon?

Both private citizens and newspapers editors rebuked Pemberton's decision in the Charleston papers. One letter published in the newspaper and simply signed "A Citizen" stated:

What, then, shall the city be given up? We suppose not. That would be indeed a qualified defense…Let the drill of the troops be at once extended to fighting in the streets and from the houses.

The governor and his council issued a warning for noncombatants to leave Charleston, though most did not. He also declared martial law and asked Pemberton and the Confederate command to enforce it. On May 5, 1862, Pemberton issued General Order No. 11, effective at noon on May 13, which affirmed martial law in Charleston and in the country up to ten miles of the city limits. Colonel Johnson Hagood, First South Carolina Volunteers, was appointed as provost marshal.

Charleston was still home to a number of citizens who were Unionists. Additionally, local authorities believed that the city was infested with Union spies who traveled in and out of Charleston. On May 12, 1862, Hagood announced that "no person will be allowed to leave the city without a written permit from the office of the provost marshal. Every person coming into the city shall report forthwith to the provost marshal."

Hagood was instructed to establish a military police force and terminate "all sales of spirituous liquors." In a proclamation, also released on May 12, 1862, Hagood announced:

That all distillation of spirituous liquors is positively prohibited and the distilleries will be closed.

The sale of spirituous liquors of any kind is positively prohibited and establishments for the sale thereof closed subject until further orders to the following regulations and regulations:

Hotels *may obtain from this department licenses to allow the use of liquors to borders at meals at the public ordinary upon terms to be specified in the license.*

Grocers *who have obtained licenses from the city authorities may, until otherwise ordered, sell liquors in quantities of not less than three gallons to any person other than those in military service or employment:* Provided, *That the same be not consumed on the premises.*

All barrooms and liquor saloons and places where liquors are retailed shall be immediately closed.

No liquor shall be sold in any quantity whatever to any soldier or person in military employment without a special license from this office.

Harriott Middleton, a spinster in her thirties, refugeed to Flat Rock, North Carolina, with her family. In writing to her cousin Susan, also a spinster, she pined, "Do you not hope that Charleston may be saved. I don't mind our house but I can't bear to give up the old streets and buildings, and churches. I feel such a strong personal love of the old place."

On May 12, 1862, the steamship *Planter* was sent to Coles Island to retrieve the four guns at the battery. Returning to Charleston in the evening, the captain decided to dock the ship at the Southern Wharf and offload the guns the next day. Defying orders of the day, the captain and white crew left the ship in the hands of a slave crew overnight, commanded by Robert Smalls, a "trusted" slave. Smalls's plan was to steal the *Planter* and turn the ship and the guns from Coles Island over to the Union blockade, seeking asylum for himself, his crew and his family.

Smalls later recorded his own account of the events that night:

Although born a slave I always felt that I was a man and ought to be free, and I would be free or die. While at the wheel of the Planter *as pilot in the rebel service, it occurred to me that I could not only secure my own freedom but that of numbers of my comrades in bonds, and moreover, I thought that the* Planter *might be of some service to "Uncle Abe." I was not long in making my thoughts known to my associates, and to my dear wife…*

I reported my plans for rescuing the Planter *from the Rebel Captain to the crew (all colored) and secured their secrecy and cooperation. On May*

13, 1862, we took on several large guns at the Atlantic Dock. At evening of that day the Captain went home, leaving the boat in my care, with instructions to send for him in case he should be wanted. As I could not get my family safely on board at the Atlantic Dock, I took them to another dock, and put them on board a vessel loading there, the Ettaone.

At half past 3 o'clock in the morning of the 14th of May 1862, I left the Atlantic Dock with the Planter, *went to the* Ettaone, *took on my family, and several other families, then proceeded down Charleston River* [Cooper River] *slowly. When opposite Fort Johnson I gave the signal and on reaching Fort Sumter at 4 A.M. I gave the signal which was answered from the fort, thereby giving me permission to pass. I then made speed for the* [Union] *blockading fleet. When entirely out of range of Sumter's guns, I hoisted a white flag, and at 5 A.M. reached a Union blockading vessel, commanded by Capt. Nichols, to whom I turned over the* Planter.

Captain Nichols was the commanding officer of the USS *Onward*. Unsure of the *Planter*'s intentions and concerned that it might be a blockade runner, he positioned his port guns on the approaching ship. Smalls came alongside the *Onward* and turned over his ship. A Union crew was placed on the ship

The crew of the USS *Unadilla*, serving as part of the Union blockade of Charleston. *Courtesy of the Library of Congress.*

and steamed for Port Royal, where Smalls was taken to Du Pont. Debriefing Smalls, Du Pont learned of the Confederate evacuation of Coles Island. The Union gunboats *Pembina* and *Ottawa* were dispatched to the Stono River and confirmed the evacuation.

The white captain, mate and engineer of the *Planter* were arrested in Charleston. The captain and mate were convicted and sentence to serve time and pay a stiff fine. While Pemberton was furious over the loss of the Planter and the dereliction of the crew, he remitted the sentences and released the two mariners.

Hunter and Du Pont agreed to a joint army-navy operation on James Island by moving up the Stono River. The general plan formulated by Gillmore for Sherman was adopted to place a significant force on James Island and march across the island to take Fort Johnson. The capture of Fort Johnson would isolate Forts Sumter and Moultrie, effectively giving the Union command control of the inner harbor.

Governor Pickens admonished that the coming Federal attack would surely be by water, since by late May, the malaria season was arriving. He assured Pemberton, "It is too late in the season for the enemy to send any land forces to invest Charleston regularly." The governor, however, was wrong.

After receiving Du Pont's report, Welles briefed President Lincoln:

> *From information derived chiefly from the contraband Pilot, Robert Smalls, who has escaped from Charleston, Flag Officer Du Pont, after proper reconnaissance, directed Commander Marchand to cross the bar with several gun-boats and occupy Stono* [River]. *The river was occupied as far as Legareville* [on John's Island], *and examinations extended further to ascertain the position of the enemy's batteries. The seizure of Stono Inlet and river secured an important base for military operations, and was virtually a turning of the forces in the Charleston harbor.*

In mid-May 1862, Brigadier General States Rights Gist, commander of Confederate troops on James Island, ordered the full evacuation of the island. His order stated:

> *Headquarters-Secessionville*
> *James Island May 19ᵗʰ 1862*
>
> *In accordance with authority from General Headquarters, persons having the ownership or charge of slaves on James Island will forthwith make*

preparations for the removal of such slaves beyond the limits of this command at an early day. The proper defense of this island renders this necessary. If desired, one male and one female slave may remain in charge of each settled plantation. Permits for them must be taken out from this office and they must be in readiness to move at a moments notice.

Beef cattle and sheep must not be removed from the Island, they being required for the use of the military. Owners of these or persons having them in charge will furnish these Headquarters with their number, locality, and marks or brands, such as are taken by the Government will be paid for by the Commissary. Forage not wanted by its owners will be taken, valued and paid for by the Quartermaster. All boats and flats must be taken to Charleston or to some point in the rear of the lines on this island before Friday next.

By Order
Brigadier General Gist

The Confederate authorities did not want a repeat of the incident with the *Planter* by having slaves betray the defenses to the Union army or navy. Additionally, unlike the governor, the Confederate command believed that James Island would be the preferred route when the Federal army decided to move on Charleston.

Even though Charlestonians felt the threat to the city was real and imminent, garden parties and balls were held at Forts Moultrie, Sumter and Pemberton. Charleston diarist Emma Holmes wrote of the "fruit cake and champagne...turkey, ham, and lobster" served at these galas. In writing of a wedding to be held in Charleston, she commented, "The war seems...an incentive to love."

Not everyone was taken by the excitement and gaiety of the times. Proper women in the city were shocked to learn that the cancan was danced by Beauregard's officers at a party. One Charleston spinster wrote, "[We have a] very vulgar set of men in Charleston and the...dreadful fast set of girls."

By mid-May, Union gunboats were spotted at the mouth of the Stono River. By the end of May, the Union navy had six gunboats in place. Five other gunboats and two barges served as troop transports. Union gunboats were running up the Stono River every morning firing on anything and anybody they could sight.

The James Island defensive lines, constructed in 1860–61, were the main line of defense to face a Union attack from the Stono River. The lines were a series of redans for artillery connected by rifle pits and breastworks stretching from the Mellichamp House on the eastern shore to the Royall House on New Town Creek, the western end of James Island Creek. The lines then turned parallel to the Stono River, reaching Fort Pemberton, located on the north side of the island near Wappoo Creek. At Secessionville, the Tower Battery was constructed on a peninsula formed by a creek from the Folly River.

In May 1862, Fort Pemberton was complete and fully armed. The "Tower Battery" at Secessionville, however, was still under construction, with only four guns mounted. The parapet in front of the guns was unfinished. Many thought the Secessionville battery was also poorly placed and designed. Perhaps overly concerned about Union gunboat fire from the Stono, the battery was placed so far inland that it gave away half of the island to the enemy.

On June 2, Major General David Hunter traveled with sixty-six hundred men from Port Royal to the Stono River and landed on James Island at Grimball Plantation. Over the next several days, additional Union troops arrived by transport and by crossing John's Island to reach the Stono River.

One Union officer on James Island wrote:

> *We are credibly informed that we and the rebels are the joint occupants of the same island, that the latter was strongly fortified, that James Island was the direct and substantially the only path to Charleston, that Charleston was only about eight miles away, that the rebels would without doubt interpose objection to one walking right over them or even around them.*

On June 2, 1862, Union troops made landfall at Grimball Plantation on the Stono River and quickly established positions on James Island and Sol Legare Island. This depiction was published in *Frank Leslie's Illustrated News* in 1862. *Author's collection.*

"Panic and Disaster Were Imminent"

Many residents in Charleston were panic-stricken to know that such a large Union force was on James Island preparing for attack. One resident noted, "People are moving in crowds from the city. Carts are passing at all hours filled with furniture." Even the bells at St. Michael's Episcopal Church were removed and sent to Columbia for safe-keeping. Lee, still in Virginia, wrote to Pemberton reminding him of the strategic importance of Charleston:

> *The loss of Charleston would cut us off almost entirely from communication with the rest of the world, and close the only channel through which we can expect to get supplies from abroad, now almost our daily dependence.*

On June 3, the 24th South Carolina Infantry met elements of the 28th Massachusetts, 100th Pennsylvania and 79th New York. In the skirmish, a number of Union troops and an officer were captured.

A temporary brigade, referred to as the "Advanced Forces," was organized under the command of Colonel Hagood, just relieved of his duties as provost marshal for this duty. Four of the best Confederate regiments in the Lowcountry (Hagood's First South Carolina, Steven's Twenty-fourth South Carolina, Simonton's Twenty-fifth South Carolina and McEnnery's Seventh Louisiana) were assigned for this duty. The brigade set up guards at Artillery Cross Roads (today's intersection of Fort Johnson and Secessionville Roads) and at Freer's Cross Roads. Outposts were established on James Island at the Episcopal church, at the Presbyterian church and on Battery Island Road. Skirmishes along the lines were frequent as each army probed the other.

On June 10, Pemberton ordered that a battery be placed near Grimball Plantation capable of firing on Union ships in the Stono River and Union troops at Grimball Plantation on Sol Legare Island. Hagood, commanding the First South Carolina, advanced on the Union troops with the Fourth

A skirmish on Sol Legare Island on June 3, 1862, between the 24th South Carolina Infantry and companies of the 28th Massachusetts, 100th Pennsylvania and 79th New York. *Author's collection.*

Louisiana on his right flank and the Forty-seventh Georgia on his left. The Confederate advance was stopped by both gunboat fire from the Stono and Union troops commanded by Brigadier General Horatio G. Wright. In his report, Wright noted, "The Naval vessels in the river kept up a continued fire over the heads of our men, and as their practice was excellent it must have occasioned much loss to the enemy's reserve.

In the skirmish, Union troops had sixteen casualties compared to forty-seven for the Confederates.

The Union command and the Northern press were supremely confident of the success of the coming attack. On June 9, 1862, the *New York Tribune* wrote:

> *"Doom" hangs over wicked Charleston. That viper's nest and breeding place of rebellion is, ere this time, invested by Union Arms—perhaps already in our hands. If there is any city deserving of holocaustic infamy, it is Charleston. Should its inhabitants choose to make its site a desert, blasted by fire, we do not think, many tears would be shed. Travellers of to-day are quite undecided as to the location of ancient Carthage; travellers of 2862 may be in the same doubt about Charleston.*

Hunter was stalled with his troops on the southwestern side of James Island and Sol Legare Island. He returned to Port Royal and left General Henry Benham in command, but with instructions not to advance and attack. After being shelled by Confederate artillery, Benham decided to advance, if only to capture the Confederate guns harassing him.

Benham ordered the Union troops to fall in at 2:00 a.m. on June 16, organizing them into two columns. The first column, thirty-five hundred men made up of six regiments with engineers, cavalry and artillery commanded by Brigadier General Isaac Stevens, was to serve as the assault group. The second column with thirty-one hundred troops was formed on the left under the command of Brigadier General Horatio G. Wright. The plan was for the first column to make a bayonet attack on the Tower Battery at first light.

At 4:00 a.m., the Union troops advanced, led by Lieutenant Lyons and a Negro guide. The column encountered four pickets three-quarters of a mile from the Tower Battery. Five men in the Eighth Michigan were wounded, but the pickets were captured.

Confederate colonel Thomas G. Lamar was serving as superintendent for the construction of the Secessionville battery. His crew worked into the night, trying to finish preparations should they suffer a Union attack. While

Union brigadier general Henry Benham. *Courtesy of the Library of Congress.*

the Union troops advanced, Lamar and his troops slept in place on the Tower Battery.

The Union advance placed the 8th Michigan in the front with two additional regiments. The second brigade consisted of the 79th New York (Highlanders), the 100th Pennsylvania (Roundheads) and the 46th New York. The 8th Michigan and the Highlanders were considered to be excellent regiments.

As the Union troops crossed a cotton field in front of the Tower Battery, Lamar awoke to see them just 50 yards from his position. With no time to awaken his troops, he pulled the lanyard of a Columbiad ready with grapeshot. An intense fight ensued. The peninsula came to a bottleneck just 125 yards wide in front of the Tower Battery, making it difficult for the reserves in the second brigade to advance in support.

Lieutenant Colonel A.D. Smith and the Pee Dee Battalion and the Charleston Battalion commanded by Lieutenant Colonel P.C. Gaillard rushed to support Lamar and his troops. The Eighth Michigan reached the parapet

An illustration of the Battle of Secessionville, June 16, 1862, published in *Frank Leslie's Illustrated News. Author's collection.*

of the battery but was repulsed. Colonel Lamar suffered a serious neck wound during the attack and turned command at the battery over to Gaillard.

With the second brigade, including the Highlanders, finally engaged, the Union troops made a second advance on the battery but were again repulsed. In the fierce hand-to-hand fighting that ensued, Gaillard was wounded, leaving Major Wagner in command of the Confederate position.

The Third New Hampshire and Third Rhode Island of the second column moved across a parallel peninsula separated by a creek and fired on the rear of the Tower Battery. The Charleston Battalion moved to confront that threat. Colonel McEnnery and his Fourth Louisiana also rushed to join the fight, screaming "Remember Butler!" as they charged. (Union General Benjamin "Beast" Butler had just occupied New Orleans a month earlier.)

Union Colonel Daniel Leasure with the 100th Pennsylvania Infantry would later write:

> *I advanced with the left flank of the Highlanders, cheering them to the charge, till when within about one hundred yards of the works three immense guns bellowed out a perfect cloud of grape, canister, old chains, empty porter bottles, nails and even brickets, and just cut the regiment in two…Panic and disaster were imminent every minute.*

Confederate lieutenant Iredell Jones, of the First South Carolina, recalled the action that morning:

> *The battery was contested on the ramparts in a hand to hand fight, and a log was rolled from the top to sweep the enemy from the sides of the*

An engraving published in *Frank Leslie's Illustrated News* depicting the Third Rhode Island and Third New Hampshire attempting to flank the Confederate position at the Tower Battery during the Battle of Secessionville. *Author's collection.*

> *breastwork. All credit is due to the Charleston Battalion and Lamar's two companies of artillery…But while we give all credit to our own troops, let us never again disparage our enemy and call them cowards, for nothing was ever more glorious than their three charges in the face of a raking fire of grape and canister, and then at last, as if to do or die, they broke into two columns and rushed against our right and left flanks, which movement would have gained the day, had not our reinforcements arrived.*

Finally, after three failed attacks, Benham ordered a general retreat at 9:45 a.m. Union forces suffered 700 casualties, while the Confederates had only 204. Most of the casualties occurred in front of or on the Tower Battery. The Eighth Michigan suffered casualties of one-third of their enlisted men. The Highlanders also suffered heavy losses. Lamar reported that 341 Union soldiers were buried on the field in front of the Tower Battery. After the battle, the Tower Battery was renamed Battery Lamar, in honor of Colonel Lamar.

The Northern press was stunned at the defeat. *Frank Leslie's Illustrated News* reported that Lamar had eight thousand men at Secessionville. In fact, when the battle started he had only five hundred troops.

Hunter was outraged that Benham ignored his orders and engaged the Confederates. He relieved Benham of command and ordered him to Hilton

Head, where he was arrested for disobedience of orders. Benham was sent North for court-martial, in which he was found guilty, though he later received a presidential reprieve.

Wright was placed in command of the Union troops on James Island. Not wanting to repeat the debacle at Secessionville, Hunter informed Wright:

You will not attempt to advance towards Charleston or Fort Johnson till largely re-enforced and until you receive express orders from these headquarters. Should you deem your present position untenable you will immediately make all necessary disposition for abandoning James Island.

Wright reinforced his position at Grimball Plantation but, after days, did not understand why he was not receiving further orders. In writing to Hunter at Hilton Head, he said, "I am bound to say in all frankness that I do not understand the object of the occupation at all, unless the command be sufficiently re-enforced to enable us to prosecute the attack upon Charleston."

On June 27, Wright received orders from Hunter to abandon James Island. By July 9, 1862, the evacuation was complete.

4

"COMPLETELY AT MY MERCY"

Immediately after the Battle of Secessionville, Governor Pickens wrote Confederate president Jefferson Davis lobbying for two changes. First, he wanted the batteries on Coles and Battery Islands reestablished. Second, he wanted Pemberton, a general he did not trust and rarely agreed with, to be relieved of command in Charleston. Davis responded that he preferred the military staff make the judgment about Coles and Battery Islands. Of Pemberton, he offered, "I am desirous of obliging you and would be glad to secure the services of General Pemberton elsewhere…My own confidence, however, in General Pemberton is such that I would be satisfied to have him in any position requiring the presence of an able general."

Despite the vote of confidence for Pemberton, Davis issued Special Order No. 202 on August 29, 1862, assigning Beauregard the command of the Department of South Carolina and Georgia. Pemberton was relieved of command on September 17, and Beauregard arrived in Charleston and assumed command on September 24, 1862.

Beauregard had requested a command in the West or at Jackson, Mississippi, where General Braxton Bragg was commanding the Confederate troops. Davis declared, "If the whole world were to ask me to restore General Beauregard to the command which I have already given to General Bragg, I would refuse it." Beauregard had enraged Davis in the previous year when the general suggested that Davis's interference and poor judgment "prevented the pursuit and full destruction of McDowell's army and the capture of Washington" after the first Battle of Bull Run.

General Pierre Gustave Toutant Beauregard. *Courtesy of the Library of Congress.*

With limited opportunities provided by Davis, Beauregard chose to return to Charleston. In a letter to Governor Pickens, Beauregard wrote, "As I understand it is the wish of all, people and Government, that the city be defended to the last extremity; hence, I desire to be in all respects ready to make its defense equal to that of Saragossa." Saragossa was a Spanish city twice besieged by French forces in the Napoleonic Wars, 1808–09. In a tenacious defense, the Spanish resisted the French with weeks of "street to street fighting."

After his arrival, Beauregard used the next six months to work on new shorter defensive lines on James Island and increasing the armament in the harbor forts. He deployed two ironclads, harbor obstructions, torpedoes and fire rafts in his strategy for the defense of Charleston. The Creole general also lobbied Richmond for more troops and ordnance.

Despite his continued belief that James Island was the key to Charleston, Beauregard believed the next Union attempt on Charleston would be a naval attack. He designed a harbor defense utilizing three interlocking circles of fire. Fort Sumter was the center of the first line, which also included Batteries Gregg and Wagner on Morris Island to the south and Fort Moultrie, Fort Beauregard, Batteries Bee, Marion and Marshall and four small batteries, all on Sullivan's Island. The second circle of fire included the James Island fortifications of Fort Johnson and Batteries Cheves, Wampler and Glover; Fort Ripley and Castle Pinckney in the harbor; a battery on Hog Island; and two batteries in Mount Pleasant. The final circle of fire depended on batteries in Charleston. Artillery crews placed range buoys in the harbor to aid in firing on any Union ships moving through.

One Charlestonian noted that on Sullivan's Island, "all of the houses nearly up to the church have been torn down, and batteries erected on their sites… There is also a new and very heavy battery from the Moultrie House, extending along the beach, and bearing directly on Moffett's Channel." One Confederate officer in Charleston observed, "[The] city is enveloped with earthworks, most handsomely constructed." With the Union troops withdrawn to Hilton Head, the immediate fears in Charleston were diminished. In August 1862, martial law was lifted, and bars and gambling houses were allowed to reopen.

By the fall of 1862, Welles was encouraging Du Pont to attack Charleston with his fleet. The Union blockade of Charleston, though ineffective at times, was still in place with six steamships and two sailing ships deployed in an arc thirteen miles long. Du Pont had little confidence in the arc strategy. In a letter to his wife, Du Pont suggested that the ships would "be firing into each other at the first alarm."

In October 1862, Confederate secretary of war George W. Randolph wrote to Beauregard suggesting that Du Pont would attack Charleston within two weeks. The attack did not come, but the Union fleet did maintain a strong presence at the entrance to Charleston Harbor and the mouth of the Stono River.

Beauregard ordered that the Wappoo Creek be deepened to thirteen feet to accommodate the newly commissioned gunboats:

> For the passage of gunboats—rams from the Ashley to the Stono, in order that they might operate in either river according to the circumstances; we will thus be enabled to retake possession of and hold Cole's Island, thereby doing away with the necessity of keeping so large a force on James Island as is now required for the protection of the city.

Stephen Russell Mallory was appointed Confederate secretary of the navy in March 1861, and he fully understood that the South possessed few resources around which he could build a wartime navy. Initially, he sought foreign contracts to build Confederate warships, resulting in the *Alabama* and *Florida*. Early in the war, Mallory secured contracts in Memphis and New Orleans to construct ironclad ships. Additionally, he initiated contracts with shipyards in Virginia and on the Tennessee River to convert existing ships into ironclad warships.

These contracts resulted in the construction of six ironclads—*Virginia*, *Arkansas*, *Tennessee*, *Mississippi*, *Louisiana* and *Eastport*. By the end of 1862, all six ironclads had been lost in combat, captured or purposely destroyed to prevent their capture.

In February 1861, the *Charleston Mercury* advocated the immediate establishment of a Confederate navy using foreign shipyards for construction. The article offered:

> *In creating a navy, as we will have to do, the question first to be determined is the kind of vessels we want; and since we have to commence* de novo, *let us avail ourselves of our experience on the rest of the world…We would suggest then, first, that such unfortified entrances, of sufficient importance, but which cannot be protected by earth works on shore, should be guarded by iron-clad floating batteries, made perfectly shot-proof, and mounting heavy shell guns, to be used against wooden-sided vessels…Congress should at once send experienced officers to England to contract for and supervise the building of such a number of steamers as it will see fit…It will be more expedient and economical to contract for these vessels in England and Scotland, where men accustomed to the work are to be found. With these first vessels as models we can build others, with our own mechanics.*

By August, the *Mercury* had changed its views. In an article on August 10, 1861, entitled "The Navy of the Confederate States," the writer asserted:

> *When the history of the present contest comes to be written by the historian…nothing probably will surprise men more than that, for months after the formation of a Government, the keel of not a single war steamer was laid by the Confederate States.*

On February 12, 1862, the Executive Council of South Carolina resolved:

> *That the Chief of the Military Department be directed to take steps for executing the ordinance or resolution of the Convention appropriating three hundred thousand dollars for building a Marine Battery or Ram and that he put himself immediately in communication with the Naval Commander of our coast for that purpose, and that he be also directed to enquire as to the most competent ship carpenters at Gosport Navy Yard or anywhere in the Confederate States he thinks proper, for the purpose of ascertaining a proper estimate for ten first-class Gun boats of the strongest model for our waters.*

On February 22, the Executive Council further authorized raising $200,000 "to be used to enlist seamen to man Gun Boats in the harbor and waters around Charleston." By early March, Mallory contracted with

Francis M. Jones, a Charleston shipbuilder, to construct three ironclads in Charleston. He agreed to complete the first ironclad in 90 days, a second in 150 days and a third within 200 days. Mallory authorized $120,000 to build the three vessels. The Charleston ironclads were to be constructed using John Porter's new design for a Richmond class of ironclads, a smaller version of the CSS *Virginia*.

The Richmond design called for an ironclad gunboat 150 feet long, with a beam of 34 feet and an 11-foot draft. It was intended to be armed with four guns: Brooke rifles fore and aft, and eight-inch smoothbores on the sides.

The first Charleston ironclad was to be named the *Chicora* and built by Eason & Brothers, located at 12 Columbus Street. James M. Eason, president of the company, was highly regarded for his locomotives built in the 1830s and his steam engines built in the 1850s. Eason had a Scottish lathe capable of constructing a flywheel twelve feet in diameter.

South Carolina, independent from the Confederate navy, remained committed to build its own ironclad rams, until George S. Trenholm, president of John Fraser & Company, convinced the Executive Council to support Mallory's project. Mrs. Sue L. Gelzer of Summerville, South Carolina, wrote a letter, published on March 3, 1862, in the *Charleston Daily Courier*, stating:

> *Having observed, a few days since, in the* Courier, *that the ladies of New Orleans had given an order for a "Gunboat," and also the idea suggested, to the ladies of Charleston, to emulate their example, I immediately concluded to send you my* mite, *to assist in the "good cause," and only regret it is not a larger sum. If* every *true woman, in our* beloved *State, would contribute the same amount, we would be enabled to give an order for more than* one *"Gunboat"…I most respectfully propose, then, that you should open a list for contributions, and inform the public, through the columns of your valuable paper.*

The editor of the *Charleston Daily Courier* published his own letter in the same issue, noting:

> *From the subjoined letter, it will be seen that a patriotic daughter of the Palmetto State has inaugurated a subscription, for building and equipping the gunboat* Palmetto State [also to be known as the Ladies' Gunboat]*; and we trust, indeed we know or at least predict, without apprehension or proving a false prophet, that her patriotic example will*

be numerously, nay multitudinously, followed…if every daughter of the Palmetto State, able to contribute one dollar, will do so, and that promptly, we shall not only see the proposed Gunboat, aloft, in our beautiful and impregnably fortified harbor, but a fleet of Gunboats will soon dance on its buoyant waters…At present, however, we confine ourselves to the project of building and equipping the Gunboat Palmetto State, *and we shall open a subscription list, for the purpose, at our office.*

The response to Mrs. Gelzer's challenge was immediate and profound. Businesses, banks, ladies' societies, private citizens and even the *Charleston Mercury*, the *Courier*'s rival newspaper, made donations for the Ladies' Gunboat. Donations arrived from as far away as Richmond and Atlanta. In May, Charleston ladies hosted a multi-day fair and raffle at Hibernian Hall, home to the Irish benevolent society, to raise funds for the ironclad.

Sufficient funds were raised to begin construction in mid-March. Marsh & Son, located on Concord Street, was contracted to build the *Palmetto State*. Like the *Chicora*, the Ladies' Gunboat was to be built using the plans by John Porter. Cameron & Company, located on Pritchard Street, assisted with the *Palmetto State*, working on the engines and mechanical components.

In the South Carolina Lowcountry, there were plentiful live oak, white oak and pine trees to frame the two ironclads. In the early colonial era, South Carolina live oak, with its high tensile strength and great resistance to rot, was highly sought after by New England shipyards.

The challenge for both shipyards was to locate sufficient iron to build the armor plating. Both shipyards advertised for lead but had to resort to destroying nonessential rail lines to harvest the railroad tracks. The T-rails were malleable and could be converted to armor plating. They were sent to Tredegar Foundry in Richmond and Atlanta Rolling Mill in Georgia to be reproduced in twenty-foot lengths, seven inches wide and two inches thick. When installed on the exterior sides of the gunboats, the armor rails were first laid horizontality, with a second layer installed vertically. The decks and hull, five feet below the water line, received only one two-inch layer. The gunboats were painted a pale bluish gray color, referred to as "blockader's blue."

With no properly sized engines available, used steam engines were harvested from small steamships for the *Chicora* and *Palmetto State*. These engines were insufficient to properly power the two gunboats, becoming a serious flaw that would soon become obvious.

Beyond the paid contractors, many businesses donated products for the gunboats. Evans and Cogswell, well known for printing Confederate currency, contributed paper products for the Confederate navy, including "pay books, pens, pencils, inkstands, and logbooks." John Fraser & Company and E.J. Hancock provided necessary items as well.

James H. Tomb, later to serve as the engineer for the *Chicora*, wrote of outfitting the ironclad:

> *After stating the condition of our finances to Mr. Eason, he generously gave me the authority to go ahead and fix up our steerage to suit myself…After I got through, there was everything in the way of furniture, damask curtains, spreads, and a pantry with everything but provisions.*

Flag Officer Duncan Ingraham, the senior naval officer in Charleston, selected able men to command the two ironclads under construction. Duncan tapped Commander John Tucker to command the CSS *Chicora*. Tucker was a native of Virginia and entered the U.S. Navy as a midshipman in 1826. In the Mexican War, he commanded the USS *Stomboli*. In 1855, Tucker was promoted to the rank of commander and given command of the USS *Pennsylvania*, a three-deck, 140-gun ship. Commander Tucker resigned from the U.S. Navy in April 1861, when Virginia seceded from the Union. He commanded the CSS *Patrick Henry*, a brigantine-rigged side-wheel steamer, from 1861 to 1862 in combat actions at Newport News, Hampton Roads, Norfolk and Drewry's Bluff, Virginia. He was given the command of the *Chicora* in July 1862. Tucker was called "Handsome Jack" by sailors with whom he served.

Lieutenant Commander John Rutledge was given command of the CSS *Palmetto State*. He was the grandson of his namesake, John Rutledge, first governor of South Carolina after the Declaration of Independence, signer of the United States Constitution and second chief justice of the United States Supreme Court.

Both the *Chicora* and *Palmetto State* were finished by October 1862. A festive ceremony was held with Flag Officer Duncan Ingraham; Commander John Tucker, commander of the *Chicora*; Lieutenant Commander John Rutledge, commander of the *Palmetto State*; Mrs. Sue Gelzer, whose letter and financial contribution gave life to the Ladies' Gunboat project; and General P.G.T. Beauregard on the program.

Richard Yeardon, editor of the *Charleston Daily Courier*, offered his remarks at the ceremony:

> *At this crisis, a noble spirit stirred in the bosoms of the daughters of the Palmetto State, and the project of building iron clad gunboats for the*

Photograph of a painting by C.W. Chapman of the CSS *Chicora* and CSS *Palmetto State* in Charleston Harbor. *Courtesy of the U.S. Navy Historical Center.*

defense of Charleston, originated in and emanated from their patriotism and public spirit...donations in money, plate, jewelry, works of art and ingenuity, family relics, tokens of affection, the widow's mite, and even bridal gifts, were poured forth as from a horn of plenty or an exhaustless fountain, to arm Charleston with the means of a defense....Noble boat! You now bear a name which is at once a badge and incentive of victory; you are armed and equipped to do battle in a righteous war, against an unprincipled enemy; and relying on the justice of our cause, let us hopefully and reverently commit your destiny to Him, with whom are the issues of life and death—of defeat and victory.

As the ceremony ended, the *Chicora* was also brought before the crowd, "steaming up from the lower wharves, and with colors flying, fore and aft, saluted her consort." With its addition to the festivities, the crowd cheered the *Chicora* and James Eason, the shipbuilder.

After their launch, the *Chicora* and *Palmetto State* conducted sailing tests and trials in the Cooper River and out to the Charleston bar. On December 12, the *Palmetto State* ran a successful trial on the Cooper River, making seven knots with the current but only four knots against the tide. James Tomb, the *Chicora*'s engineer, recorded, "She was thought to be able to make eight knots without forced draft, but when completed, could not under the most favorable circumstances make over seven." In fact, on one trial, the *Chicora* struggled against the outgoing tide while near Fort Sumter and had to drop its anchor to avoid being swept out to sea.

Charlestonians were proud of the two ironclad gunboats but became impatient to see them in action against the Union blockade that was causing so much harm to the Charleston economy. On January 28, 1863, the *Charleston Daily Courier* published a letter simply signed "A. Mariner":

> *Mess'rs Editors—Why is it that with—gunboats at this port well armed, manned, and officered, and, "spoiling for a fight," we do not clear the blockade? Why is it that so much material, gallant officers and men, and scientific accomplishments and preparation, should be wasted in doing nothing, and should not protect the very large and singular important trade to this port in its egress and ingress?*

Beauregard was not impressed with the capabilities of the Confederate ironclads, and he preferred the development of a design for ironclad torpedo rams. However, by late January, the time was right to test them in battle. Beauregard gave the go ahead for two daring missions on the water around Charleston.

The steam screw frigate USS *Wabash* was a constant fixture at the Charleston blockade. The forty-eight-hundred-ton ship, armed with forty Dahlgren guns, was one of the most powerful ships in the U.S. Navy. It served as Du Pont's flagship and led the attack in the Battle of Port Royal. The *Wabash* was responsible for the capture of at least five blockade runners near Charleston. In late January 1863, it temporarily pulled out of the blockade and returned to Port Royal.

Additionally, the ironclad USS *New Ironsides* had arrived in Port Royal but had not yet deployed to Charleston. The *New Ironsides* was built for oceangoing combat, perfect for facing a formidable enemy warship or capturing blockade runners. It had a complement of 449 officers and men and was armed with four Parrott rifles and fourteen Dahlgren guns.

Du Pont was also assembling ironclad monitors at Port Royal. On January 27, he dispatched the *Montauk*, *Seneca*, *Wissahickon*, *Dawn* and *C.P. Williams* to attack Fort McAllister in Georgia to test their effectiveness in combat against a masonry fortification. Beauregard assumed that they were undoubtedly brought to the South Atlantic for a future action at Charleston.

The USS *Isaac P. Smith* joined the South Atlantic Blockading Squadron in the fall of 1862 and was used to patrol the Stono River. The gunboat was formerly a steamship working the Hudson River in New York, transporting cattle on the lower deck and passengers above. Utilizing a propeller rather than a paddle wheel, the ship could run up to twelve knots. At the outbreak of the war, the Federal government commandeered all available ships, converting some to gunboats and others to transports. With its light draught and quick speed, the *Isaac P. Smith* was a perfect candidate to outfit as a gunboat. The top staterooms were stripped away, and the ship was armed with eight eight-inch guns, four to a side, and a thirty-pound gun on the bow. It was one of fifteen warships involved at the Battle of Port Royal.

It made daily morning patrols up the Stono River to harass the construction of any Confederate batteries along the river and capture or destroy any blockade runners attempting to use the "back door" to Charleston Harbor through the Stono and Wappoo Creek. On its patrols, it steamed just close enough to fire on Fort Pemberton, near the Wappoo Creek.

After firing on Pemberton, Lieutenant Conover, commanding the *Isaac P. Smith*, usually steamed back down the Stono River and anchored. The officers would go ashore to the Paul Grimball Plantation on John's Island, amusing themselves with target practice on charcoal figures drawn on the Grimball barn.

Confederate lieutenant colonel Joseph A. Yates, First South Carolina Regular Artillery, stationed on James Island, grew increasingly irritated with the arrogance of the *Smith*'s patrols. His first plan to end the Union navy's dominance on the Stono was to load armed troops onto approach barges and approach the *Smith* at night using the element of surprise to overtake its crew and seize command of the ship. However, Yates abandoned these plans in favor of a bolder attack that would take careful planning and execution. He discussed his plan with Brigadier General Roswell S. Ripley, who forwarded the idea to General Beauregard. Initially, Beauregard thought the success of Yates's plan was unlikely, but in late January, he approved the mission.

Yates placed Captain F.H. Harleston at Legare's Point Place on the James Island shore commanding three companies, each armed with a twenty-four-pound rifle gun. Company A, commanded by Lieutenant W.G. Ogier; Company B, commanded by Lieutenant E.B. Calhoun; and Company C, commanded by Captain T.B. Hayne were to move their guns into place, keeping them covered with brush in the day. Sharpshooters from the

Twentieth South Carolina Volunteers commanded by Captain J.C. Mitchell were also assigned to Harleston's station.

Farther up the James Island shoreline, Major J. Webman Brown established a battery with two rifle guns and sharpshooters from a Georgia battalion. Major Charles Austin Jr. was given command of several field guns and a detachment of sharpshooters dispatched to the Grimball Plantation on John's Island. Austin had gun platforms built in abandoned slave cabins and placed his field guns behind a garden wall under a grove of live oaks and another hidden in the carriage house. During preparations, Yates had his men running cold camps with no campfires or hot rations that could be detected by the enemy.

On Friday, January 29, rather than the traditional morning run up the Stono River, the *Isaac P. Smith* was taking on supplies from a "beef boat" at Stono Inlet. Yates and his men became distressed as the day passed without any sign of the Union gunboat. Finally, late in the afternoon, Lieutenant Commander Bacon, aboard the Union gunboat *Commodore McDonough*, dispatched the *Isaac P. Smith* up the Stono River. The gunboat was normally manned with a crew of 56 men, but on this day Lieutenant Conover made the trip with 119 officers and men aboard. As was his usual practice, Conover had a runaway slave familiar with the waters of the Stono to pilot his ship. Sailors perched in the crow's nest of each of the *Smith*'s three masts serving

Harper's Weekly engraving of the USS *Isaac P. Smith*. *Author's collection*.

as lookouts. Conover himself was scouting both the James and John's Islands shorelines, looking for any activity.

At 4:30 p.m., Lieutenant Gardner rode along the shoreline to alert the awaiting Confederate batteries, though by that time, the *Isaac P. Smith* was already abreast of the Grimball Plantation before the gunners could get into position. Only by crawling through a ditch behind a cassina hedge could the Confederates get into position. The Union gunboat passed them heading upriver before they could get ready. Surprisingly, none of the lookouts spotted the Confederate troops and field guns at Grimball Plantation.

Instead of moving all the way to fire on Fort Pemberton, Conover anchored just above Grimball Plantation and within range of the Confederate field guns. Yates waited twenty minutes to see if a landing party would depart the ship for John's Island. After no such landing appeared imminent, the guns at Grimball Plantation opened fire.

The *Smith* fired a broadside, and Union sharpshooters made ready. Conover ordered the crew to slip the cable to the anchor and to fire up the boiler to make a quick departure. At that moment, the James Island batteries opened fire, placing the *Isaac P. Smith* in a crossfire. The Confederate guns were finding their mark, and sharpshooters were picking off sailors aboard ship. The pilot was killed, and one artillery round left a hole in the steam chimney. The *Smith*'s boiler was hit three times, and its power was gone. Conover considered blowing up his own ship to prevent its capture, but with wounded men all over the deck and left with a defenseless ship, he had no choice but to hoist a white flag of surrender up the rigging.

Hearing the intense firing, the *Commodore McDonough* steamed up the river to rescue the *Isaac P. Smith*. Seeing the surrender, the ship considered trying to sink the *Smith* with its powerful bow gun to prevent its capture. However, almost running aground and worried about other hidden batteries that may be unleashed, the rescue ship turned back to Stono Inlet.

The *Isaac P. Smith* suffered twenty-five casualties, while only one Confederate artilleryman was lost. Lieutenant Conover and the wounded and remaining crew of the *Isaac P. Smith* were removed and taken prisoner. Lieutenant Colonel Yates invited his officers to join him as he took dinner that night in the wardroom of the Union gunboat. Yates reported to General Beauregard:

> *I never enjoyed a meal more fully than that I took in the* Smith*'s ward room…She has good beef, which we had not had for months, fresh vegetables, some luxuries, including a little wine, and luxury of luxuries, a table with a white tablecloth and plenty of dishes.*

"Completely at My Mercy"

The next morning, the steamer *Sumter* towed the *Isaac P. Smith* to Fort Pemberton. Later, the captured prize was taken farther up the Stono River to the Wappoo Creek to be pulled into Charleston. The guns from the Union gunship were distributed to batteries in the Lowcountry, including James Island Batteries Pringle, Tynes and Cheves. The Union gunboat was refitted and christened as the CSS *Stono* under the command of Captain Henry J. Hartstene, providing guard duty in Charleston Harbor. The capture of the USS *Isaac P. Smith* is the only time a warship was captured by ground forces only.

While Yates and his men were executing their plan, the Union blockading ships captured perhaps the biggest prize of the entire war. The British *Princess Royal*, a blockade runner, was attempting to make a high-speed run into Charleston Harbor. Its cargo included two new powerful steam engines purchased for two ironclads now under construction in Charleston. It also carried a large supply of rifled guns, small arms and ammunition. The USS *Unadilla* and USS *Housatonic* gave chase, causing it to run aground. On January 30, they refloated the British ship and held it in capture. One Union officer referred to the capture as the "war's most important single cargo of contraband."

Commodore Ingraham briefed Tucker and Rutledge on the plan to test the Charleston ironclads against the blockading ships. They hoped to recapture the *Princess Royal* before it could be removed to be sold at a Federal prize court.

In preparation for the attack, the crews coated the gunboats' armor with grease, thinking this might help deflect any enemy shells. At 10:00 p.m. on the night of January 30, Ingraham boarded the *Palmetto State*, making it his flagship. At 11:30 p.m., the *Palmetto State* left the dock with the *Chicora* following. Three small steamers—*General Clinch*, *Chesterfield* and *Etiwan*—were waiting near Fort Sumter to serve as tenders for the two ironclads.

Slowly steaming past Fort Sumter and toward the Charleston bar, William H. Parker, executive officer aboard the *Palmetto State*, would later write of the trip on the ironclad:

> We steamed slowly down the harbor, and knowing we had a long night before us, I ordered the hammocks piped down…As there was no necessity for preserving quiet at this time the captain let them enjoy themselves in their own way…after midnight the men began to drop off by twos and threes, and in a short time the silence of death prevailed…visiting the lower deck, forward, I found it covered with men sleeping in their pea-jackets peacefully and calmly; on the gun-deck a few more of the thoughtful seamen were

pacing quietly to and fro, with folded arms; in the pilot-house stood the Commodore and Captain, with the two pilots; the midshipmen were quiet in their quarters (for a wonder), and aft I found the lieutenants smoking their pipes, but not conversing. In the ward-room the surgeon was preparing his instruments on the large mess-table; and the paymaster was, as he told me, "lending him a hand."

With full ordnance and crew, the Confederate ironclads were too heavy to cross the bar and had to wait for high tide. By 4:00 a.m., the tide was high enough for them to pass. Anchored just beyond the shipping channel were the Union blockading ships: the *Mercedita, Keystone State, Quaker City, Ottawa, Unadilla, Augusta, Stettin, Flag, Memphis* and the flagship *Housatonic*.

All of the Union ships in the blockade were wooden steamers and lightly armed. Charlestonians were most familiar with the *Memphis*. It was built in Scotland and worked as a blockade runner in and out of Charleston. On June 22, 1862, it ran aground trying to enter Charleston Harbor with a cargo from Nassau and was captured by the USS *Magnolia*. The Union navy purchased it at a prize court in New York and recommissioned it as the USS *Memphis*. The *Stettin* was also formerly a blockade runner, captured on May 24, 1862, by the USS *Bienville* while trying to enter Charleston Harbor with a cargo of lead, quinine and saltpeter, a form of potassium nitrate used in the manufacture of gunpowder.

As the *Palmetto State* steamed toward the *Mercedita*, its crew mistook the Confederate ironclad for a blockade runner. The *Mercedita* had just returned from giving chase to a blockade runner, and Captain H.S. Stellwagen was resting in his quarters. When the lookout hailed the approaching ship, someone answered, "This is the Confederate States steamer *Palmetto State*." Parker recalled the confrontation:

As we approached the bar, about 4 A.M., we saw the steamer Mercedita *lying at anchor a short distance outside it…we went to quarters an hour before crossing the bar, and the men stood silently at their guns…they did not see us until we were very near. Her captain hailed us, and ordered us to keep off or he would fire…we struck him on the starboard quarter, and dropping the forward port-shutter, fired the bow gun. The shell from it, according to Captain Stellwagen who commanded her, went through her diagonally, penetrating the starboard side, through the condenser, through the seam-drum of the port boiler, and exploded against the port side of the ship, blowing a hole in its exit four or five feet square.*

After suffering both the ram and the point-blank fire of the Brooke rifle, the *Mercedita*'s crew was panicking. One crew member wrote, "Shot through the boiler! Fires putout—gunner and one man killed and a number fatally scalded—water over fire-room floor—vessel sinking fast!" In his report, Lieutenant Commander Abbot, executive officer aboard the *Mercedita*, noted:

> *Within two minutes she* [Palmetto State] *was into us…no gun on the ship could be depressed or trained to hit her, though every effort was made, she being so low in the water…we had only time to get the watch to quarters, and before we could slip our cable we were without steam.*

With no alternative after the crippling attack, Stellwagen surrendered to the *Palmetto State*.

Abbott was received on the Confederate ironclad to discuss the surrender terms with Commodore Ingraham. Without other ships to tow the *Mercedita*, Ingraham could not take the wooden steamer as a prize. Instead, he offered Abbott a pardon if he would "give his word of honor, for his commander, officers and crew, that they would not serve against the Confederate States until regularly exchanged." Abbott agreed to the terms and was returned to his ship.

The *Chicora* moved on the steamer *Keystone State*. Commander William E. Le Roy on the Union blockader was obviously aware of the attack on the *Mercedita*, and he fired on the *Chicora* as it approached. Tucker, commanding the *Chicora*, responded with his guns. One shot from the *Chicora* pierced the *Keystone State*'s steam drum, scalding an officer and nineteen men to death and wounding twenty others. This damage to the steam drum left it partially disabled in the water.

Tucker, in his report, recorded that the *Keystone State* "was completely at my mercy…I gave the order to cease firing upon her and directed Lieutenant

A *Harper's Weekly* engraving of the CSS *Palmetto State* and CSS *Chicora* attacking the USS *Mercedita* and USS *Keystone State*. *Author's collection.*

Bier, first lieutenant of the *Chicora*, to man a boat and take charge of the prize; if possible, to save her. If that was not possible, to rescue the crew." The *Keystone State* lowered its colors, a long-standing tradition in the navy to indicate surrender. However, Captain Le Roy later said he lowered his colors "out of pity for the dying and the dead." Bier, continued in his report, "The *Keystone State*, not only struck her flag on the morning of January 31, but we saw a number of her men rush upon the after-part of her deck and extend their arms towards us in an imploring manner."

Tucker recorded in his report:

> *While the boat was in the act of being manned I discovered that she was endeavoring to make her escape by working her starboard wheel, the other being disabled, her colors down. I at once started in pursuit and renewed the engagement. Owing to superior steaming qualities she soon widened the distance to some 200 yards. She then hoisted her flag and commenced firing her rifled guns, her commander, by this faithless act, placing himself beyond the pale of civilized and honorable warfare. The* Keystone State *did not surrender, rescue or no rescue, and her escape ought probably to be regarded as a rescue.*

Tucker and his crew clearly believed Le Roy violated proper protocol of naval combat. In his report to Du Pont, Le Roy made no reference to lowering his colors, saying "before our wheels entirely stopped we were able to get a hawser from the *Memphis* and were taken in tow." However, in his ship's log, Le Roy confided, "The ship being helpless and the men slaughtered…I ordered the colors to be hauled down." He then asserted, "Finding the enemy was still firing upon us, I directed the colors to be rehoisted, and resumed our fire from the after battery."

In the two actions, the *Mercedita* and *Keystone State* suffered forty-seven causalities. There were no casualties on the two Confederate ironclads. Searching for additional targets, the Confederates fired on the *Housatonic*, *Quaker City* and *Augusta*, causing some damage but no casualties. One shot on the *Augusta* pierced its starboard side, passed just above the boiler and lodged in the port side. One shot from the *Chicora* hit the *Quaker City*, piercing its hull seven feet above the waterline and exploding in the engine room.

The Union fleet pulled anchor and steamed south with the *Princess Royal*. The *Keystone State* was towed by the *Memphis*. The *Chicora* and *Palmetto State* were far too slow in open water to pursue the Union ships, and Ingraham broke off the attack at 7:30 a.m.

At 8:00 a.m., the Confederate ironclads moved to the Beach Channel near Fort Moultrie and anchored to wait for high tide so they could cross the bar. At 4:00 p.m., the two ironclads moved into Charleston Harbor as heroes. One resident described the jubilation in the city as "almost equal to the day of the Battle of Fort Sumter." Beauregard immediately sent word to Ingraham, writing, "Permit me to congratulate you and the gallant officers and men under your command for your brilliant achievement of last night, which will be classified hereafter with those of the *Merrimack* and *Arkansas*."

That same day, Beauregard and Ingraham released a proclamation:

> *At about the hour of 5 o'clock this morning the Confederate States naval forces on this station attacked the United States blockading fleet off the harbor of the city of Charleston, and sunk, dispersed, or drove off and out of sight for the time the entire hostile fleet. Therefore, we, the undersigned, commanding, respectively, the Confederate States naval and land forces in this quarter, do hereby formally declare the blockade by the United States of the said city of Charleston, S.C., to be raised by a superior force of the Confederate States from and after this 31st day of January, 1863.*

Under international law, once a blockade was broken, a thirty-day grace period had to be observed before it could be reestablished. In the afternoon, Beauregard took the French and Spanish consuls out to the bar to witness that the U.S. government had vacated the blockade. The British consul sailed out on the HMS *Petrel*, anchored at Charleston, to witness the same. That night, the French, Spanish and British consuls met with Captain Watson, commanding officer of the HMS *Petrel*, and decided the "blockade was legally raised as claimed by the proclamation."

The proclamation was wired to Confederate secretary of state Judah Benjamin, and he immediately informed the foreign consuls in Richmond. Benjamin then sent a letter by ship to James M. Mason and John Slidell in London to present the proclamation to Earl Russell, British minister of foreign affairs. By the time the letter arrived, Russell had already been informed of the resumption of the blockade, and he did not accept the proclamation.

The Union ships waited beyond the horizon, about seven miles out, until the evening. The *Mercedita* sailed for Port Royal. The *Keystone State* followed, still under tow by the *Memphis*. The *Augusta* was sent to Port Royal posthaste to inform Du Pont of the attack. The other Union ships steamed back to the mouth of Charleston Harbor to resume the blockade. Though contrary to international law, the Federal government never recognized that it had abandoned the blockade.

On Tuesday, February 3, 1863, the Charleston community turned out en masse to a victory ceremony held at St. Philip's Episcopal Church.

When informed of the attack and the poor showing of his blockading fleet, Du Pont immediately dispatched the USS *New Ironsides* to Charleston. Later, his ironclad monitors were sent to Charleston as well to neutralize the threat of the Confederate ironclads. The *Chicora* and *Palmetto State* were no match for the Federal monitors, which carried armor twice as thick and more powerful guns. Du Pont maintained a presence with the ironclad monitors at Charleston until the end of the war.

5

"THE TURRETS
ARE COMING"

In 1863, Union brigadier general Truman Seymour made a reconnaissance of the outer harbor at Charleston. He recommended to General Hunter that troops be deployed to Morris Island, capture Battery Wagner and then use breeching batteries on Morris Island and the Union fleet to capture Fort Sumter. Hunter received but did not act on Seymour's recommendations.

In February 1863, Washington sent ten thousand troops, commanded by Major General John G. Foster, to Hilton Head for operations against Charleston. Foster favored Gillmore's plan of operations against Morris and Sullivan's Islands, setting up a conflict between Hunter and Foster.

Du Pont was being pressured by Assistant Secretary of the Navy Gustavus Fox to move on Charleston. In writing Secretary of the Navy Gideon Welles, Du Pont suggested that Fox "overrates the monitors as much as he underrates the defenses" of Charleston. Du Pont, in assessing a naval attack on Charleston, referred to the harbor as "a good deal like a porcupine's hide and quills turned outside in and served up at one end." Relying on intelligence gathered from Confederate deserters and escaped slaves, he did not have an accurate measure of the firepower assembled in Charleston Harbor or the challenge of moving through the swift currents in the channel.

Lincoln met with his naval and army commanders in Washington to discuss the progress of the war. Foster once again pitched his proposal to capture Charleston by first taking Morris Island. Lincoln expressed his concern that approaching by Morris Island could result in a protracted siege. Like Welles and Fox, the president favored a naval attack, hoping to bring a swift capture of Charleston.

Fox was dispatched by Welles to meet with Du Pont at Port Royal. Fox suggested to Du Pont that with a large show of force by the monitors, he should "go in and demand a surrender of the forts or the alternative of destruction to their city." Despite his misgivings about the monitors, by March 1863, Du Pont had assembled seven monitors, the USS *Keokuk* and the USS *New Ironsides*, totaling thirty-two guns. He also ordered rafts to be built on the bow of the monitors to clear any obstructions or torpedoes they might encounter in Charleston Harbor, though he expressed, "I have no more idea that we can use them than we can fly."

On April 5, 1863, the Federal squadron and support ships assembled off the Charleston bar. The *Keokuk* buoyed the channel finding sufficient depth for the Union ships. Du Pont planned to pass the outer Confederate batteries and move to fire on the north and west faces off Fort Sumter. After forcing the Confederate fort's surrender, the monitors, supported by the wooden steamers *Canandaigua*, *Housatonic*, *Unadilla*, *Wissahickon* and *Huron*, would attack Confederate fortifications on Morris Island.

Beauregard issued an order for noncombatants to leave Charleston in the face of the pending attack, but Charlestonians were supremely confident of victory and few left. Frank Vizetelly, a correspondent for the *Illustrated London News*, was in Charleston. Prior to the attack, he filed a report with the London newspaper, writing:

> I have every faith in the result of the coming encounter, for never at any time have the Confederates been more determined to do or die than they express themselves now. Every preparation has been made, every appliance pressed into service by General Ripley, the Brigadier commanding, to give the foe a warm reception; and, surrounded as he is, apparently by obstacles that appear insurmountable, his zeal and success seem perfectly wonderful. His head-quarters during the coming fight will be in Fort Sumter itself, and, as he expresses it, he will "fight it low down" until not a brick nor stone is left for another to rest upon before he gives in. If the mail-clad monsters now in the offing are repulsed, it will be to General Ripley and the brave men under him that victory will be due.

Vizetelly wrote that the pending attack would "assuredly be one of the most extraordinary ever witnessed—amour-plated ships against sand-batteries, earth works, and brick and stone forts." He received permission to join Rhett and the garrison at Fort Sumter.

The morning of April 7 was clear, and seeing the movement of Du Pont's monitors, Confederate colonel Alfred Rhett at Fort Sumter telegrammed the city announcing, "The turrets are coming," referring to the pillbox turrets on top of the monitors. Charlestonians assembled in great numbers at the Battery and on the rooftops and steeples to watch the naval attack.

Du Pont organized his gunboats in two divisions, with the *New Ironsides*, serving as his flagship, in the middle.

Colonel Alfred Moore Rhett, Confederate commander of Fort Sumter, April to September 1863. *Courtesy of Willis J. Keith.*

FIRST DIVISION

SHIP	GUNS	COMMANDER
Weehawken	2 guns	Captain John Rodgers
Passaic	2 guns	Captain Percival Drayton
Montauk	2 guns	Captain John L. Worden
Patapsco	2 guns	Captain Daniel Ammen

FLAGSHIP

New Ironsides	16 guns	Captain T. Turner

SECOND DIVISION

Catskill	2 guns	Commander G.W. Rodgers
Nantucket	2 guns	Commander D. McN. Fairfax
Nahant	2 guns	Commander John Downes
Keokuk	2 guns	Commander A.C. Rhind

Du Pont admired Rodgers as a daring and talented officer and chose him to lead the attack. Captain Percival Drayton, commander of the *Pocahontas* in the Battle of Port Royal, was chosen to command the *Passaic* and follow

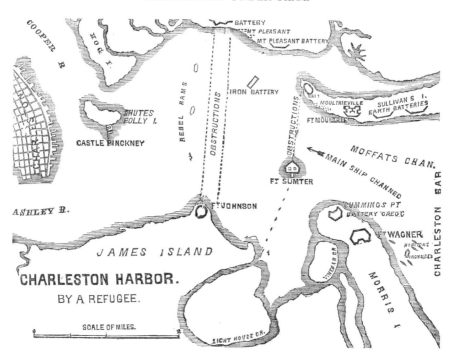

Above: A map of Charleston Harbor drawn by a refugee noting the positions of the Confederate batteries and the obstructions placed in the shipping channel. *Author's collection.*

Left: Union naval officers on the turret of the USS *Passaic*. *Courtesy of the Library of Congress.*

Rodgers. Drayton was the son of a most prominent South Carolina family, but at the war's outset, he determined to stay in the U.S. Navy. Captain Worden, commander of the *Montauk*, commanded the *Monitor* in the now-infamous ironclad battle with the CSS *Virginia* at Hampton Roads in 1862.

Du Pont held his ships back until high tide at 10:20 a.m., thinking the outgoing tide would aid in steering the monitors. The Union ships began moving just after noon, but the advance stalled as the *Weehawken*'s anchor became tangled with the torpedo-protection raft on its bow. The advance resumed at 1:45 p.m.

Frank Vizetelly boarded a small transport to travel to Fort Sumter and, passing the Battery, was fascinated to see the walls filled with Charlestonians waiting to see the attack. He sketched the scene and wrote that "the ladies of Charleston had no undue fear for the result of the attack, which, if successful, would place their homes at the mercy of an exasperated foe."

By 2:30 p.m., the Confederate garrison at Fort Sumter, finished with its midday supper, was called to the guns. The Confederates were attired in their dress parade uniforms, excited to finally face the Union fleet in battle. The fort's band played as the Palmetto, garrison and South Carolina First Artillery flags were raised over the fort. Colonel Alfred Rhett, commander at Fort Sumter, fired a thirteen-gun salute and prepared to face the oncoming ships.

When the *Weehawken* came within range, Fort Moultrie opened fire, hitting the ship's turret and the side of the ironclad at the waterline. The *Passaic* fired first on the bellowing guns at Fort Moultrie as the *Weehawken* opened fire on Fort Sumter. As the *Weehawken* passed a range buoy, all the guns at Fort Sumter and on Sullivan's and Morris Islands opened fire, though at the long range, the first shots did little damage.

The *New Ironsides*, with its flat bottom, was having trouble in the channel. This caused great confusion in the Union battle group. The *Catskill* and *Nantucket* collided with *New Ironsides*, now sitting still. As the *New Ironsides* drifted, it passed over a Confederate mine, though the mine did not detonate. The massive mine was designed to be fired from the shore, but when engineer Langdon Cheves tried to detonate it, nothing happened. In his report, Cheves offered, "For ten minutes he could not have placed the *Ironsides* more directly over it if he had been allowed to, but the confounded thing, as usual, would not go off when it was wanted."

Du Pont and Turner signaled to the other ships to ignore the movement of the flagship and move to the attack. Water spray and drifting smoke created by the many shots hitting and landing near the *Weehawken* left the

An illustration of the April 1863 ironclad attack on Fort Sumter, published in *Harper's Weekly. Author's collection.*

ship's pilot and gunners blind. A mine exploded near the *Weehawken*, causing more consternation for Rodgers and his crew. The *Weehawken* was under intense fire for forty minutes, and the effective shots destroyed much of its armor and pierced its deck.

The *Passaic* managed to fire thirteen shots but was hit thirty-four times by Confederate fire. One shot struck the turret and ricocheted to hit the pilothouse. The intense fire and damage forced the *Passaic* to retire for repairs.

The slow, cumbersome monitors were no match for all the Confederate guns. Captain Worden, in his report of the action, noted that "the accuracy of the shooting on the part of the rebels was very great." The Confederate artillerymen were using "a new device invented by Lt. Colonel Joseph A. Yates, 1st South Carolina Artillery, that allowed guns to be trained to follow the moving ships and remain on target. This was a forerunner of modern fire control systems." Yates was also the mastermind behind the plan that captured the USS *Isaac P. Smith* on the Stono River.

The guns at Fort Sumter continued firing at a quick pace. By 3:35 p.m., the *Catskill*, *Nantucket*, *Nahant* and *Keokuk* had navigated around the *New*

"The Turrets Are Coming"

Officers on the deck of the USS *Catskill*. *Courtesy of the Library of Congress.*

Ironsides and moved to within nine hundred yards of Fort Sumter. After only the third shot fired, the *Nantucket* had one gun disabled.

The *Nahant* suffered the heaviest fire from the guns at Fort Sumter. After only getting off fifteen shots, its turret became jammed and its steering failed, causing it to drift dangerous close to the Confederate guns. At close range, Confederate shots were shearing off bolts and rivet heads on the ironclad. The pilot and quartermaster were wounded, leaving only Commander Downes in the pilothouse of the damaged monitor. Finally, the crew managed to repair the steering, and the *Nahant* quickly retreated before it was destroyed.

One seaman aboard the *Catskill* revealed, "Officers and men were astonished to see the injuries done to these supposed invulnerable ironclads." Inside the monitors, "the nuts that secured the laminated plates flew wildly, to the injury and discomfiture of the men at the guns." A reporter traveling with the Union fleet observed that the shots from Confederate guns "literally rained around them, splashing the water up to thirty feet in the air, striking and booming from their decks and turret." All of the ironclads were suffering damage that, in many cases, disabled the ships or jammed their turrets.

The *Keokuk* made a direct approach to Fort Sumter, leaving its broadside vulnerable to Confederate fire from both sides of the channel. Its guns were out of commission after only firing three shots. Additionally, Commander Rhind was having great trouble handling his monitor in the swift current. It was hit ninety times; nineteen of those shots either pierced the hull or hit below the waterline. Its light armor could not adequately protect the ship.

C.W. Whitey, the designer of the *Keokuk*, boldly asserted that his new ironclad featured a shot-proof design. His boasting rang hollow as the crew worked hard to plug the holes in the ship. Rhind had to withdraw to prevent the complete destruction of his ship.

The *New Ironsides* remained a mile away from the action. Captain Turner made one attempt to move in closer but quickly found that he was receiving the attention of all the Confederate guns. Ninety shots hit the *New Ironsides*, while it only managed to fire seven ineffective shots on Fort Moultrie.

After the great battle, Vizetelly wrote:

> *The engagement...lasted two hours and twenty-five minutes...There were eight turreted ironclads, including the boasted double-turreted* Keokuk *and an immense plated frigate known as the* Ironsides. *All these marine monsters were armed with eleven and fifteen inch guns. They were all struck*

An engraving from the *Illustrated London News* of the *New Ironsides* firing on Fort Sumter. *Author's collection.*

by the forts repeatedly; and after maintaining the fight for the time I named, they steamed away, evidently much damaged. This morning we have ample evidence of the fact…Clothes clotted with blood have been picked up that floated from the Keokuk, *and there can be little doubt that she was pierced through and through, and that the loss of life on board her has been severe…The Confederate loss does not amount to more than four men killed and about a dozen wounded. There were a few casualties here* [Fort Sumter] *and we had two of our guns dismounted by the fire from the ships. The fight may be renewed at any moment if the Federals have the stomach for the attempt; but I think they have suffered too much to provoke another encounter.*

Now facing an incoming tide that could cause his ships to drift into close range of the Confederates, Du Pont signaled all of the monitors to withdraw at 4:30 p.m. The Union ships ceased fire and started steaming away, but the Confederate guns continued their fire until the enemy was out of range.

Once out of range and at anchor, the Union commanders all met on the *New Ironsides* to make their reports. In the two-and-a-half-hour battle, the Union monitors only managed to fire 154 rounds, and only 34 of them hit their target. The Confederate batteries and Fort Sumter fired 2,209 rounds, with 520 of them hitting Union ships. Five of the ironclads suffered enough damage to either disable the ship or its guns. Though the ships were heavily damaged, the Union force only had twenty-three casualties.

One Union officer observed that the *Keokuk* was "riddled like a colander." The ship retired fourteen hundred yards south of Morris Island while its crew continued to work to plug the many holes and leaks. The next day, when the wind picked up creating a rough sea, the *Keokuk* sank.

Again, the next morning, Du Pont met with his senior officers aboard his flagship. Everyone agreed that the attack should not continue for a second day. Du Pont assured them he did not want to turn "failure into disaster." In his report to Washington, he wrote, "I attempted to take the bull by the horns, but he was too much for us. These monitors are miserable failures where forts are concerned." While en route to Port Royal, Du Pont wrote to his wife, confiding, "We have failed as I felt sure we would."

Some of the Union shots left craters in Fort Sumter's walls two and a half feet deep, but overall, the damage to the fort was minimal. Thirty-four shots from the monitors hit the walls of the fort, fifteen of them causing damage. The Confederate casualties only totaled four dead and ten wounded, most of them in an accidental explosion on Morris Island.

A *Harper's Weekly* illustration of the sinking of the USS *Keokuk*, drawn by a Union naval officer. *Author's collection.*

When the monitors departed the next day, Rhett held a victory dress parade at Fort Sumter and fired another thirteen-gun salute. The *New Ironsides* remained with the blockade ships, perhaps to discourage another attack by the Confederate ironclads.

Du Pont ordered the Union ships to destroy the sunken *Keokuk*, but the rough seas prevented them from doing so. The Union officers were certain they could not salvage the *Keokuk*'s guns and felt they could prevent the Confederates from making a similar attempt. On April 19, Major D.B. Harris, Beauregard's chief engineer, and General Ripley visited the site of the sunken ship. Assessing the opportunity, they believed the large Dahlgren guns could be recovered.

Adolphus W. LaCoste, a civilian employee in the Ordnance Department, was assigned the task of salvaging the guns, no small task given their weight of eight tons each. The first task was to remove the top of the *Keokuk*'s turrets, a job that took two weeks. With the *Chicora* and *Palmetto State* providing escort for the salvage crew, the first gun was recovered on May 2. Three nights later, the second gun was recovered from the wreck of the *Keokuk*. One Dahlgren gun from the *Keokuk* was mounted at Fort Sumter and the other at Battery Bee on Sullivan's Island.

The defeat of the heralded Union monitors was a great embarrassment for the Union navy. The Northern press reacted harshly. The *New York Herald* described the defeat, "though almost bloodless, as one of our most discouraging disasters." President Lincoln and Secretary Welles worked to delay the official reports of the battle to the public. Welles expressed to Du Pont that his reports were not published

> *because in my judgment, duty to my country forbade it. They may justify the failure at Charleston ad excuse your abandoning, after a single brief effort, a purpose that the nation had at heart, and for which the department had, with your concurrence and supposed approval, made the most expensive and formidable preparation ever undertaken in this country.*

Du Pont responded with his own letter, once again, justifying his withdrawal.
On July 3, 1863, Du Pont received a letter from Welles, stating:

> *From the tone of your letter it appears that your judgment is in opposition to a renewed attack on Charleston, and in view of this fact, with your prolonged continuance on the blockade, this Department has concluded to relieve you of the command of the South Atlantic Squadron.*

Rear Admiral John A. Dahlgren was dispatched to South Carolina to replace Du Pont.

6

"MEN FELL BY THE SCORES"

While Du Pont prepared his attack, Major General Hunter had established a foothold on Folly Island. In a letter sent directly to Lincoln following the ironclad attack, Hunter wrote:

> *On the day of that attack, the troops under my command held Folly Island up to Lighthouse Inlet. On the morning after the attack we were in complete readiness to cross Lighthouse Inlet to Morris Island, where once established, the fall of Sumter would have been as certain as the demonstration of a problem in mathematics.*

In truth, during Du Pont's attack, Brigadier General Seymour had urged Hunter to cross the inlet and attack, but he responded that he "thought the attempt was too hazardous." Hunter was relieved of command in June 1863, replaced by Brigadier General Quincy A. Gillmore.

Gillmore revived his old plan for the capture of Charleston written when he was chief engineer for General Sherman. He planned to capture the southern end of Morris Island, eliminate Battery Wagner and destroy Fort Sumter, thus allowing the Union navy to reach the inner harbor of Charleston and force the city's surrender.

Union brigadier general I. Vogdes commanded a brigade holding Folly Island. Most of the island was "very thickly wooded, the undergrowth being dense and almost impassable." On the east end of the island, where the island was narrow, Vogdes established pickets along Lighthouse Inlet.

The ruins of the blockade runner *Ruby* can be seen on Folly Island, where it ran aground passing the Federal blockade squadron on June 11, 1863. *Courtesy of the Library of Congress.*

General Henry W. Halleck, Lincoln's general in chief, questioned the approach over Morris Island versus attacking through James Island. Gillmore wrote in response, "The answer is simple. The enemy had more troops available for the defense of Charleston than we had for the attack." Gillmore, however, was wrong. He had 11,500 troops assembled on Folly and Seabrook Islands ready to assault Charleston, while Beauregard only had 5,841 troops to defend the region. The defeat at Secessionville in 1862 left the Union army overcautious about traversing James Island to capture Charleston.

Beauregard anticipated that the Union army would move from Folly Island to Morris Island and, from there, attempt to capture Fort Sumter. He assessed, "They will find that to be a piece of folly."

Morris Island was a large sand island on the western side of the channel into Charleston. The island was three and three-quarters miles long and ranged from twenty-five to one thousand yards wide. The largest Confederate fortifications were Batteries Gregg and Wagner. Battery Gregg was located on the northernmost tip of the island at Cumming Point.

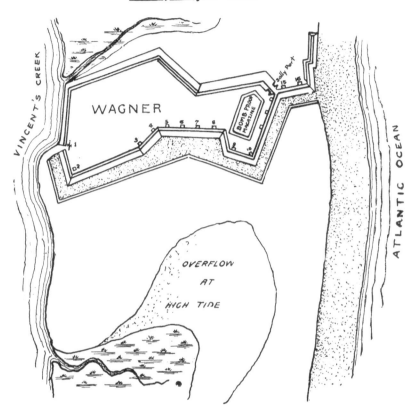

SKETCH OF BATTERY WAGNER, 1863.—J. H.

1. Fieldpiece. 2. 10″ Mortar. 3 and 4. Carronades. 5. 32 dr. 6. 8″ Navy.
7. 32 dr. 8. 8″ Navy. 9. 32 dr. 10. 8″ Howitzer. 12. 32 dr. Rifled.
13. 10″ Columbiad. 14. 8″ Gun. 15 and 16. 12 dr. Field Howitzers.

An 1863 sketch of Confederate Battery Wagner. *Courtesy of Willis J. Keith.*

Approximately three-quarters of a mile south of Battery Gregg was Battery Wagner. Wagner was strategically located at the narrowest part of the island where only 25 yards of sand separated the marsh on the west and the ocean on the east. One Confederate officer wrote of the battery, suggesting "nature designed this spot for defense, and there is no other site of the Island equal to it." Just beyond the marsh, 250 yards in front of Battery Wagner, was a sand ridge, a perfect location for pickets and sharpshooters.

Before Pemberton was removed from command in Charleston, he ordered construction of Battery Wagner. It was first appropriately referred to as the

Union general Quincy Gillmore in front of his tent on Morris Island. *Courtesy of the Library of Congress.*

"Neck Battery" but was later named Battery Wagner in honor of Lieutenant Colonel Thomas Wagner of the First Regiment, South Carolina Artillery, who was killed at Fort Moultrie. Work was completed on Battery Wagner by June 1863.

When Beauregard learned that Gillmore had replaced Hunter, he decided to write to the Union general to express his hopes for the gentlemanly and appropriate conduct of the Union army in the coming fight. On July 4, 1863, Beauregard, in a lengthy letter, wrote, "In the interest of humanity, it seems to be my duty to address you, with a view of effecting some understanding as to the future conduct of the war in this quarter."

Beauregard continued to detail acts committed by the Union army while commanded by Hunter that he regarded as violations of the established rules of warfare. These violations included the burning of Bluffton, South Carolina; the destruction and looting of Darien, Georgia; and the burning of Jacksonville, Florida. Beauregard acknowledged, "You have, of course, the right to seize and hold our towns…but not to ravage and destroy the houses or other property of the individuals of the country."

Beauregard quoted and directed Gillmore's attention to the *Law of Nations*, written by Swiss legal philosopher Emmerich de Vattel in 1758. Vattel's work guided the work of the American founders when drafting the United States Constitution. His guidelines pertaining to the proper conduct of war were long regarded as a guideline for civilized nations.

Beauregard asserted that to destroy or ravage the country of one's enemy and attack noncombatants was, in the words of Vattel, the "result of hatred and fury…Savage and monstrous excess…the belligerent who wages war in that manner must justly be regarded as carrying on war like a furious barbarian." He ended by saying:

> *In conclusion, it is my duty to inquire whether the acts which resulted in the burning of the defenseless villages of Darien and Bluffton, and the ravages on the Combahee, are regarded by you as legitimate measures of war, which you will feel authorized to resort to hereafter.*

Beauregard addressed the letter to Gillmore in Port Royal and delivered it to the blockade ships off the coast of Charleston. At the time, Gillmore was already on Little Folly Island, preparing to attack Morris Island.

Gillmore launched two diversionary attacks prior to his assault on Morris Island. The first attack was led by Colonel Thomas W. Higginson commanding the First South Carolina Volunteers, a regiment of escaped South Carolina slaves formed in January 1863. They were to move against a railroad bridge on the Edisto River at Jacksonborough, disrupting the Charleston and Savannah Railroad. The attack failed. The second diversion was thirty-eight hundred troops commanded by Brigadier General A.H. Terry landing on the southwestern side of James Island. A Confederate attack forced Terry's troops to retire to the protection of the gunboats on the Stono River.

Early in the morning of July 9, a Confederate scouting party observed Federal troops preparing barges in Lighthouse Inlet. Early on July 10, the Union troops pulled away brush and cut trees to expose forty-seven guns, which fired on the Confederate position on the south end of Morris Island. Dahlgren, aboard the *Catskill*, with the *Nahant*, *Montauk* and *Weehawken*, moved close to shore to add their firepower to the attack.

After three hours of combined army and navy gunfire, two thousand Union troops from the Third New Hampshire, Sixth and Seventh Connecticut, Ninth Maine, Seventy-sixth Pennsylvania and Forty-eighth New York landed on Morris Island, dislodged the Confederate troops there and secured the southern end of Morris Island for Gillmore. There were seven hundred Confederate troops to defend the attack. They suffered casualties totaling 42 percent of their troops and lost eleven guns.

With the Union troops now on Morris Island, the monitors moved close to Battery Wagner. After taking on strong and effective fire, the monitors

The Union camp on the south end of Morris Island in early July 1863. *Courtesy of the Library of Congress.*

retreated, but not before the *Catskill* suffered sixty hits. The Confederate forces retreated to the safety of Battery Wagner.

The next day, Gillmore ordered an attack on Battery Wagner, thinking he could quickly overwhelm the sand fort. Four companies of the Seventh Connecticut, supported by the Seventy-sixth Pennsylvania and the Ninth Maine, made the assault. The Union troops suffered 339 casualties in a fierce fight with the Confederates before they withdrew. The Confederates only had 12 casualties in Battery Wagner.

Brigadier General Strong's report of the action on July 11 indicated that

> the Seventy-sixth Pennsylvania halted and lay down upon the ground… The causes of their failure, and hence the failure of the assault, were, first, the sudden, tremendous, and simultaneous fire which all encountered, and second, the absence of their colonel, who was taken ill before the column was put in motion.

A captain in the Seventh Connecticut was bitter in his assessment of the supporting regiments, saying they "broke and fled."

Over the next six days, Gillmore established four Union batteries with a total of forty guns on Morris Island. On June 16, the *Charleston Daily Courier* reported: "A forest of masts present themselves to our view just outside the bar, mortar boats, gunboats, and monitors, lie within range of our guns on

Morris Island." The Confederate command understood that another attack on Battery Wagner was imminent.

Battery Wagner held a garrison of thirteen hundred men commanded by Brigadier General William B. Taliaferro. Positioned within the sand fort, the Charleston Battalion, commanded by Colonel Palmer C. Gaillard, held the right. Gaillard and his men were battle-tested veterans from the Battle of Secessionville in 1862. The Fifty-first North Carolina, commanded by Colonel H. McKethan, held the center, and the Thirty-first North Carolina, commanded by Lieutenant Colonel Charles W. Knight, held the left side, closest to the ocean. There were also two companies of Sixty-third Georgia Heavy Artillery and two companies of the First South Carolina Infantry, acting as artillery.

On July 18, at 10:00 a.m., the Union batteries opened an intense bombardment of Battery Wagner, firing an average of fourteen shells per minute. Dahlgren moved five monitors, five gunboats and the *New Ironsides* to add their guns to Gillmore's batteries firing on Battery Wagner. After ten continuous hours of bombardment, firing more than nine thousand shells, Gillmore ordered a second infantry attack on Battery Wagner.

The firing was so intense that Confederate troops sought cover in bombproofs, on the parapets, in "ratholes" (buried rice casks) and anywhere they thought they could seek cover. Most of the guns at Wagner were disabled, and the Confederate artillerymen ceased their return fire. The Confederate troops were exhausted from the daylong bombardment and the extreme heat and poor air in the bombproofs. Many of those inside Wagner had had little sleep since the July 10 assault. One Union soldier wrote, "No one would suppose that a human being, or a bird even, could live for a moment upon that fort."

Gillmore placed Brigadier General Thomas Seymour, formerly with Major Anderson at Fort Sumter, in command of six thousand troops organized into three brigades. The attack would be led by Brigadier General George C. Strong commanding six regiments in the first brigade. The second brigade, with four regiments, was commanded by Colonel Haldiman S. Putnam, and Brigadier General T.G. commanded the third brigade. Putnam did not agree with the plan for the frontal assault, and he commented to a junior officer that "we are going into Wagner like a flock of sheep."

At the urging of Colonel Robert Shaw, Strong assigned the Fifty-fourth Massachusetts the "post of honor" to lead his brigade. He asserted, "It was believed that the Fifty-fourth was in every respect as efficient as any other body of men; and as it was one of the strongest and best officered, there seemed to be no good reason why it should not be selected for the advance." The Fifty-fourth Massachusetts was the first black regiment recruited in the North. The officers were all white, chosen from wealthy families prominent in the abolition movement.

Just before the attack, Shaw instructed Lieutenant Colonel Hallowell, saying, "I shall go in advance with the National flag. You will keep the State flag with you; it will give the men something to rally around. We shall take the fort or die there!"

Strong rode up to address Shaw's men:

> *Boys, I am a Massachusetts man, and I know you will fight for the honor of the State. I am sorry you must go into the fight tired and hungry, but the men in that fort are tired too. There are but three hundred behind those walls, and they have been fighting all day. Don't fire a musket on the way up, but go in and bayonet them at their guns.*

Strong then looked at the color bearer, asking his black troops, "If this man should fall, who will lift the flag and carry it on?" Shaw quietly responded, "I will," to the resounding cheers of his men.

At dusk, the six hundred men of the Fifty-fourth Massachusetts led Strong's brigade in the attack. They were supported by the Ninth Maine and Seventy-sixth Pennsylvania in the main column, the Sixth Connecticut on the right flank and the Third New Hampshire and Forty-eighth New York on the left flank.

As they neared the battery, a massive fire poured forth from Wagner. Wagner's fire was supported by Confederate guns from Fort Sumter, Battery Gregg and James Island.

All of the Confederate troops in Battery Wagner moved into action with the exception of the Thirty-first North Carolina. The Thirty-first refused to exit its bombproof, leaving the left salient of the battery undefended. This allowed troops from the Sixth Connecticut and Forty-eighth New York to enter Wagner.

With the first brigade experiencing heavy losses, Putnam's brigade was ordered to advance, but he stalled for fifteen minutes before complying. Shaw, climbing the rampart at Wagner, challenged his men to "Forward, Fifty-fourth!" He was quickly killed. The troops from the Fifty-fourth Massachusetts who followed Shaw to the top of the parapet were all killed. Others broke ranks and fled back to the beach. Shortly, other than Captain Little with the Seventy-sixth Pennsylvania, all of the commanding officers in the first brigade were either killed or wounded.

When the second brigade stalled, this left the surviving men of the Sixth Connecticut and Forty-eighth New York without support. They were quickly engaged in hand-to-hand fighting as the Charleston Battalion moved over to defend the left flank. Though the Confederates were successful, Captain Ryan of the Charleston Battalion was killed.

All of the Union troops obeyed the order to remove the caps from their guns and make a bayonet charge except the 100th New York, in the second brigade. Colonel Dandy insisted that his men "never fired without orders." When the second brigade reached the moat in front of Wagner, however, it lost its composure and fired a volley, only to shoot the 3rd New Hampshire and 48th New York. One Union soldier later wrote, "Men fell by the scores on the parapet and rolled back into the ditch; many were drowned in the water, and others smothered by their own dead and wounded companions falling upon them."

Once the second brigade did engage, additional Union troops were able to enter the fort on the left salient. Word was sent for Stevenson's brigade to advance and join the fight, but it never arrived. Brigadier General Johnson

An illustration, published in *Harper's Weekly*, of the Federal attack on Battery Wagner, July 18, 1863. *Author's collection.*

Hagood arrived with the Thirty-second Georgia to reinforce Wagner, and they helped repulse the Union troops who made it inside the battery.

A general retreat was ordered for the Union troops, but many of those who had penetrated the Confederate battery were still engaged in fierce hand-to-hand combat. This continued for another three hours until the Union troops in the battery were killed, wounded or captured.

An officer with the Third New Hampshire was wounded and trying to make his way to the rear. As he moved down the beach, he witnessed "a sickening sight. It was of several unfortunate men lying upon the beach, some dead and others dying, the rising tide slowly but surely drowning those that lived."

Lieutenant Daniel West, Sixth Connecticut Infantry, later wrote:

> *I had been in several battles before in Virginia…but nothing in my experience compared with the slaughter in front and in Fort Wagner that night…The dead and wounded covered it* [the seaward wall] *so that it was impossible to get around. All of our commanding officers were either killed or disabled.*

By 10:30 p.m., that attack was over, leaving a horrific scene in its wake. Vizetelly was at Battery Wagner to witness the fight. He reported to his readers:

> *All through the night we could hear the screams and groans of the wounded lying within a few yards of us; but as a continual fire was kept up by the advanced pickets it was impossible to do anything for them without running great risk of being shot. Early in the morning, however, the Federals sent a flag of truce, asking for a cessation of hostilities, that they might bury their dead. The first demand was granted, but they were told they could not be permitted to come within the lines of the Confederates and the latter would perform the last offices for the fallen enemy. In the ditch they lay piled, Negroes and whites, four and five deep on each other; there could not have been less than 250 in the moat, some partially submerged; and altogether over 600 were buried by the Southerners.*

A soldier in Battery Wagner with the Thirty-second Georgia Infantry described the scene on Sunday morning:

> *I never saw such a sight as presented itself on Sunday morning at day brake* [sic]*—as far as the eye could reach could be seen the dead and*

dying on all sides…I never saw such a sight, men with heads off, many with legs shot off.

A reporter for the *Charleston Daily Courier* wrote, "Probably no battlefield in the country has ever presented such an array of mangled bodies in a small compass as was seen on Sunday morning."

General Strong was wounded during the attack on Battery Wagner. While in the hospital, he spoke of the Fifty-fourth Massachusetts, saying, "The 54th did well and nobly. Only the fall of Colonel Shaw prevented them from entering the fort. They moved up as gallantly as any troops could, and with their enthusiasm, they deserved a better fate." Strong died of tetanus on July 30.

The Union army suffered more than 1,500 casualties, including 111 officers. The Fifty-fourth Massachusetts suffered the highest casualties at 272 officers and men. Strong's first brigade suffered one half of the total Union casualties. The Confederate casualties only totaled fewer than 200. With the exception of the Thirty-first North Carolina, the troops in Battery Wagner defended the fort beyond anyone's expectations.

Beauregard was elated with the victory. On the morning of July 19, he telegrammed General Joe Johnston in Brandon, Mississippi, writing:

Praise be to God! The anniversary of Bull Run has been gloriously celebrated. After shelling Battery Wagner all day yesterday…[the] *enemy attempted to storm Battery Wagner last night, but was gallantly repulsed with great slaughter.*

He forwarded copies of the message to General Braxton Bragg in Chattanooga, Major General W.H.C. Whiting in Wilmington and Brigadier General H.W. Mercer in Savannah.

This second defeat at Battery Wagner forced Gillmore to rethink his plan, and he prepared for siege operations on Morris Island. A palisade was constructed on the southern end of Morris Island to protect Union troops against any advance by Confederates at Battery Wagner.

On July 20, Gillmore finally responded to Beauregard's letter of July 4, in which he questioned the intended conduct of the Union troops at Charleston. Gillmore was displeased that Beauregard's letter was delivered through the blockade fleet. He clearly was angry that the naval officers were aware that the Confederate commander was lecturing him. Gillmore tersely wrote:

A Federal camp on Morris Island in the summer of 1863. *Courtesy of the Library of Congress.*

It was a source of no little surprise to me that your communication [July 4 letter] *was sent by way of the blockading fleet off Charleston, while our respective pickets on this island are within speaking distance of each other…I respectfully suggest that hereafter communications for me, to which my attention is at all desirable, be sent through my own lines.*

In addressing Beauregard's admonishments about the proper conduct of war, Gillmore responded:

Passing over without comment, as purely irrelevant, your severe strictures upon certain military operations of my predecessor commanding this department, I will simply state that, while I shall scrupulously endeavor to conduct the war upon principles well established by usage among civilized nations, I shall expect from the commanding general opposed to me a full compliance of the same rules.

Beauregard was incensed at Gillmore's letter, and he quickly responded, noting:

I am quite at a loss to perceive the necessity of your remark that you "will expect from the commanding general opposed" to you "full compliance with the same rules"…inasmuch as I am wholly unaware that there has been any departure on my part, or by any of my troops, from the established laws and usages of war between civilized peoples.

Regarding the method of delivery of his first letter, Beauregard jabbed at his opponent by offering, "I had believed you would naturally prefer that route [through the navy] for flags of truce, inasmuch as it was clearly the one least calculated to interrupt your operations for the reduction of Battery Wagner."

Beauregard published their letters in the Charleston newspaper, knowing that everyone, North and South, would see the exchange. The *Sumter* (South Carolina) *Watchman* republished the letters in its newspaper and offered, "Beauregard uses up the Yankee General with his pen, and if he can do the same with his sword we shall rejoice."

The Northern press was also carefully watching the jousting between the two formidable generals. The *Boston Journal* wrote, "The contest now going on at Charleston between two of the best, if not absolutely the two best, engineers in their respective armies, is extremely interesting in every point of view."

The Boston newspaper continued to assess the situation in Charleston by offering:

> *In the present struggle Gillmore has displayed decided superiority over Beauregard in one respect—that is, in getting a foothold on Morris Island. If he had been kept out of that—and he might have been—he could have made no progress.*

The Northern press was not alone in its critique concerning Gillmore's ability to secure a foothold on Morris Island. Though pleased with the two Union defeats at Battery Wagner, President Davis expressed his own concern that Beauregard "allowed" Gillmore to cross to Morris Island. Confederate secretary of war James A. Seddon, on behalf of Davis, wrote to Beauregard questioning his choice of strategy for defending Charleston.

Beauregard quickly responded that he intended to provide a lengthy, detailed report of the actions in Charleston; however, he felt compelled to immediately address the concern expressed. Beauregard reminded the secretary that he was required to defend Charleston from at least three approaches. He noted that on James Island he had only 2,906 men when he had previously notified the War Department he required 11,500 for an adequate defense. Likewise, on Morris Island, he initially had 927 men, instead of the 3,000 requested, and on Sullivan's Island there were only 1,158 troops rather than the 3,500 requested. Beauregard added that he only had 870 troops to hold in reserve in Charleston.

His letter continued with an assessment of Gillmore's assets:

> *The force of the enemy may be set down as at least four brigades, of 2,500 men each, or a total of some 10,000 men, with ample means of transportation and every appliance of war, supported by the guns of a powerful and numerous fleet.*

Beauregard continued his response by highlighting one of his chief complaints since returning to Charleston:

> *It may be asked, why was not this catastrophe guarded against? To which I would say, generally, that stronger works could not be erected for lack of labor, though every effort was exhausted to secure negroes from the day I took command of the department up to July 1, 1863. Further, I had not been able to get the armament essential for such works, and, besides, as before said, I did not have a garrison sufficiently strong for Morris, James, and Sullivan's Islands at the same time. The holding of the position [Morris Island] is secondary to that of James Island, which must be secured beyond peril, if possible, of surprise and capture.*

William Porcher Miles, Confederate congressman from South Carolina, also wrote to Seddon defending Beauregard's choices and reminding the secretary of the limitations of resources in Charleston. Miles had previously expressed his concern that Charleston was being "stripped of troops against the earnest remonstrance of General Beauregard, in order to re-enforce General Johnston." He maintained that "the enemy took advantage of our weakness to attack us when we could not have a sufficient force of infantry on Morris Island to effectually resist them."

Miles concurred with Beauregard that James Island, not Morris Island, had to be given the primary attention. He cited, "The possession of James Island by the enemy would be virtually the possession of Charleston. The possession of Morris Island is but a distant step to that end." Miles also reminded Seddon that both Generals Lee and Pemberton, before Beauregard, "addressed themselves almost exclusively to the defense of James Island and paid little attention to the defense of Morris Island." Like Beauregard, Miles reiterated the point that Charleston had far fewer troops than needed for the defense of the city.

On July 20, Gillmore opened fire on Battery Wagner from two newly constructed batteries. Gillmore also ordered the Union batteries on Morris

Island to turn their attention to Fort Sumter. Dahlgren's fleet turned its guns on Morris Island and Fort Sumter as well. By late July, Dahlgren had four monitors, the *New Ironsides* and seventeen ships inside the bar. Additionally, there were thirty ships in the Folly River and one gunboat and four ships in the North Edisto River. They were still holding one frigate, one sloop of war, one gunboat and thirty-four troop transports at Hilton Head.

Beauregard and his district engineer, Lieutenant Colonel D.B. Harris, planned to fill the casemates at Fort Sumter with wet sand and bales of cotton soaked in salt water to support the walls. The work on-site was supervised by Lieutenant John Johnson, the engineer at the fort. Beauregard also transferred twenty of Fort Sumter's guns to James Island and around the inner harbor defenses. Colonel Alfred Rhett, Confederate commander at Fort Sumter, prepared his garrison for the attack they assumed would come.

On August 17, 1863, Union Battery Brown fired on Fort Sumter with two eight-inch Parrott rifles, one firing solid shot and the other percussion shells. Other batteries joined in, bringing eighteen guns to bear on Fort Sumter. By midmorning, the monitors *Passaic* and *Patapsco* had joined in the attack. In the first twenty-four hours of the Fort Sumter bombardment, one thousand artillery rounds were fired by the Union army and navy. At Fort Sumter, seven guns were disabled and the walls suffered heavy damage.

Officers of the USS *Philadelphia*, flagship of the South Atlantic Blockading Squadron, posing aboard ship with a twelve-pound Dahlgren gun mounted on a field carriage. *Courtesy of the Library of Congress.*

A Union mortar crew ready for action on Morris Island. *Courtesy of the Library of Congress.*

The intense bombardment of Fort Sumter continued each day. The walls of Fort Sumter could not withstand the force of the heavy rifled Parrott guns Gillmore was using for the bombardment. By August 21, the Confederate guns at Fort Sumter were not returning fire. From August 17 to August 23, more than fifty-six hundred shots were fired on Fort Sumter.

During this bombardment, Union troops began a slow advance on Battery Wagner by digging zigzag trenches, though the Confederates harassed them daily with fire from the guns at Wagner and their sharpshooters.

As the trenches advanced, the Union soldiers made some gruesome discoveries. Many of the Union and Confederate troops killed in the July 10 and July 18 assaults on Fort Sumter were buried in mass graves where they fell. One officer commanding a trenching crew reported:

> *A very unpleasant feature connected with this…arose from the number of dead bodies found in all our advanced works…Ten have been exhumed in one night. Handling these bodies was very disagreeable…many soldiers, friend and foe, were wrapped in blankets only, and others not that.*

Union soldiers on Morris Island use the sap roller, a large cylinder filled with sand, to provide cover from sharpshooters at Battery Wagner to allow them to dig trenches, advancing on the Confederate stronghold. *Courtesy of the Library of Congress.*

On August 21, the Union troops made an unsuccessful attack on the rifle pits positioned in front of Battery Wagner. Again, in the late afternoon of August 24, Wagner received the full attention of the Union guns and Dahlgren's fleet. At dusk, the Union troops once again tried to storm the pickets and rifle pits, but, like three days earlier, they were repulsed.

7

"A Swamp Angel
Will Preach"

The civilian noncombatants in South Carolina were feeling the effects of the second year of the blockade. One Charlestonian fleeing the city wrote to her cousin, asking, "Has it ever occurred to you to turn envelopes…I am determined to buy nothing I can possibly do without, and I hear that letter paper in all shapes is at a fabulous price." Her cousin in Columbia wrote back, "Living is getting hard here too, meat we have given up, it is so very bad when you can get it, and poultry we only remember." Susan Middleton, in writing to her cousin Harriott, complained, "We have not had potatoes for months, and regard them as a first class luxury, entirely beyond our reach."

While the Union army had established a foothold on Morris Island, they were still too far from Charleston to be able to fire directly on the city. Gillmore felt that if he could shell Charleston, he would weaken the resolve of the Confederates and force a surrender of the city.

Gillmore asked Colonel Edward Serrell of the First New York Engineers to find him a spot between Morris Island and James Island to build a battery to reach Charleston. Colonel Serrell sent a lieutenant from the engineer corps to look for available sites. The young engineer reported that the mud was generally more than twelve feet deep and could not support the weight of a man.

The engineer reported back to Serrell that constructing a battery in the marsh was impossible. Legend has it that Serrell was most displeased with the lieutenant's attitude and ordered him to get the job done and requisition the materials he needed. The exasperated lieutenant promptly requisitioned twenty men eighteen feet tall to do the job. He then requested that the regimental surgeon splice three six-foot men together to give him his eighteen-foot-tall man.

Serrell did finally locate a spot of high ground between Morris Island and Lighthouse Creek that was twenty-five to thirty feet long and fifteen to eighteen feet wide. After seventeen days of testing and planning, Serrell finally had a design for the battery to submit to General Gillmore. On July 16, Serrell, in his report to the assistant adjutant general, acknowledged that the marsh could be "crossed by infantry at low tide, with some difficulty." He also noted that the construction crews would have to cross a creek approximately nine feet wide. Serrell estimated that a large Parrott gun, elevated thirty-five to thirty-seven degrees, could fire a shell five and a quarter miles, a distance that would reach Charleston from the proposed location.

Serrell built a "trial platform" elsewhere on marsh mud to test his calculations for the weight and support of the gun site. On August 2, he submitted his construction plans to Gillmore. His crew laid a foundation of cut marsh grass over the proposed site. On top of the grass, Serrell laid two thick canvas tarpaulins. Next, he installed a pine grillage and poured sand through the crevices. This formed the basic gun platform.

The actual gun platform was going to have to support twenty-four thousand pounds of gun and carriage. Once completed, the platform required twenty thousand feet of wooden planking cut from the pine forest on Folly Island, six hundred pounds of iron spikes and the equivalent ten thousand man-days of labor. Sergeant Fitter of the New York Engineers remarked, "We're building a pulpit on which a Swamp Angel will preach." The name "Swamp Angel" stuck, but this was meant to be an angel of death for those in Charleston.

During construction, picket boats with bow howitzers and sharpshooters were staged nearby to protect the construction crew. Union soldiers carried more than thirteen thousand sandbags weighing over eight hundred tons across a wooden plank causeway that was two feet wide and seventeen hundred feet long.

With the platform complete, the 8,000-pound gun carriage was moved through the marsh to the site. A 200-pound Parrott rifled gun, weighing 16,300 pounds, was then moved through the marsh to the awaiting platform. It took all night to float the gun by boat to the site and another four days to mount the gun. Shells, powder and primers were delivered, while Union captain Nathaniel Edwards took compass readings on St. Michael's steeple. The gun was elevated to an angle never before used for the large shells to be fired by the Parrott gun.

A thief is being drummed out of the Union camp on Morris Island in the summer of 1863 in this "Rogue's March." *Courtesy of the Library of Congress.*

With his "angel" ready for action, Gillmore sent a dispatch to Beauregard demanding "the immediate evacuation of Morris Island and Fort Sumter… within four hours [or]…I shall open fire on the City of Charleston from batteries already established within easy and effective [range] of the heart of the city." When the dispatch arrived at Confederate headquarters, Beauregard was away inspecting defenses in the city. Further, Gillmore's demand was unsigned, and Beauregard's aides returned it to the Union lines for verification.

With no response from Beauregard, Gillmore proceeded with his plans to bombard Charleston. While the city had a number of legitimate military targets and the city's moored blockade runners, he was also well aware of the presence of many civilians still in the city.

On the night of August 21, Frank Vizetelly was settled in his hotel room reading about the Battle of Waterloo. Crossing into the hours past midnight, he was lying awake in his bed when the Swamp Angel fired the first shot at 1:30 a.m. on August 22. He described the shot as resembling "the whirr of a phantom brigade of cavalry in mid-air."

An intense explosion threw him toward the window. Looking out, he could see smoke and fire in the building across the street. Knowing that never before had a shell traveled the distance between the city and the Union

War correspondent Frank Vizetelly of the *Illustrated London News* sketched this scene of the first shot fired from the Swamp Angel landing in Charleston. *Author's collection.*

positions, he considered that "a high meteor had fallen." Minutes later, a second shot was fired into the city nearby.

Running downstairs to the lobby, Vizetelly encountered "terrified gentlemen" who had traveled to Charleston to purchase black market goods referred to as "blockade cargoes." He observed that they rushed about "in the scantiest of costumes and the wildest alarms."

Vizetelly wrote of that night:

> *One perspiring individual of portly dimensions was trotting to and fro with one boot on and the other in his hand, and this was nearly all the dress he could boast of. In his excitement and terror he had forgotten the number of his room from which he had hastened at the first alarm, and his distress was ludicrous to behold. Another, in a semi-state of nudity with a portion of his garments on his arm, barked the shins of every one in his way in his efforts to drag an enormous trunk to the staircase. On reaching the hall I found a motley crowd, some of whom with the biggest of words were cursing the Federal commanders. Whirr! Came another shell over the roof, and down on their faces went every man of them into tobacco-juice and cigar-ends and clattering among the spittoons. I need not say that this is a*

class of men from whom the Confederacy hopes nothing; on the contrary, by their extortion, practiced on a suffering people, they have made themselves execrated. If a shell could have fallen in their midst and exterminated the whole race of hucksters, it would have been of great benefit to the South.

The population was now aroused, the streets filled with women and children making their way to the upper part of the city, where they would find comparative safety. The volunteer fire-brigades brought out their engines, and parties of the citizen reserves were organized rapidly and quietly, to be in readiness to give assistance where required. The first engine that reached the house struck by the first shell was one belonging to a Negro company, and at it they went with a will, subduing the fire in a marvelously short time. At every successive whirr about them the niggers shouted quaint invectives against "cussed bobolitionists," scattering for shelter until the danger was passed. Through the streets I went, and down to the Battery promenade, meeting on my way sick and bed-ridden people carried from their homes on mattresses, and mothers with infants in their arms running they knew not whither. Reaching the promenade, I cast my eyes towards the Federal position, and presently beyond James Island, across a marsh that separates it from Morris Island, came a flash, then a dull report and, after an interval of some seconds, a frightful rushing sound above me told the path the shell had taken; its flight must have been five miles!

During the bombardment, Vizetelly met his friends Captain Scheibert and Captain Ross in the hotel bar. The three Europeans passed the time by placing bets on the next landing location of each successive Federal shell. Captain Ross would write of their ludicrous game in which he offered Vizetelly "a thousand to one that a shell we heard coming would not hit either of us." The English reporter accepted the bet, "forgetting that if he won he would have had but a small chance of realizing his wager—and, of course, I won my dollar."

After two hours of constant shelling, the firing slowed and, near dawn, stopped. That night, a total of sixteen shells were fired into Charleston. The Union gun crew used 25 percent more powder than normal to ensure that the shells reached the city. Ten of the shells were laced with "Greek fire," an incendiary chemical that was an early form of napalm. Panic was widespread in the city. The residents could not fathom how the Union guns could reach Charleston. Exhausted, Vizetelly and many of the other guests at the hotel went to bed.

Beauregard immediately dispatched a letter to Gillmore the next morning. He informed his adversary that the letter demanding evacuation that was sent for verification was not returned to Charleston until 9:00 a.m., after a night of shells fired into the city.

A *Harper's Weekly* engraving of the Swamp Angel battery firing on Charleston. *Author's collection.*

Incensed, Beauregard wrote:

> *Among nations not barbarous the usages of war prescribe that when a city is about to be attacked timely notice shall be given by the attacking commander, in order that non-combatants may have an opportunity for withdrawing beyond its limits. Generally the time allowed of from one to three days; that is, time for withdrawal, in good faith, of at least the women and children. You, sir, give only four hours, knowing that your notice, under existing circumstances, could not reach me in less than two hours, and that not less than the same time would be required for an answer to be conveyed from this city to Battery Wagner…*
>
> *It would appear, sir, that despairing of reducing these works* [Batteries Gregg and Wagner and Fort Sumter], *you now resort to the novel measure of turning your guns against the old men, the women and children, and the hospitals of a sleeping city, an act of inexcusable barbarity.*

Beauregard concluded his letter, noting, "I am taking measures to remove, with the utmost celerity, all non-combatants, who are now fully aware of and alive to what they may expect at your hands."

Gillmore acknowledged Beauregard's letter but refused to concede that the city did not receive sufficient notice of his intent. Gillmore noted:

> *I am led to believe that most of the women and children of Charleston were long since removed from the city, but, upon your assurance that the city is still "full of them," I shall suspend the bombardment until 11 p.m. tomorrow.*

That morning, the English, French and Spanish consuls sent personal letters to Gillmore asking that the resumption of firing on the city be delayed. The Spanish consul wrote:

> *The short termination of your notification is not sufficient in order that the subjects of S.M. Catolica place in safety their lives and personal effects. The city so soon, in its lower part, deserted by its inhabitants, was not so completely that the bombardment did not fail to have some innocent victims.*

H. Pinckney Walker, "Her Majesty's Acting Consul," wrote Gillmore as well and requested a meeting. Gillmore responded that taking the time to meet with him would interfere with his operations, and he declined the request.

Many people left Charleston to join friends or families at plantations in the country parishes. However, as Vizetelly reported, "there were hundreds whose circumstances compelled them to remain."

The shelling of Charleston resumed on the evening of August 23. After the nineteenth shot, the gunner notified Lieutenant Sellmer that the gun's jacket had moved and he could not get his primer down in the gun. Concerned that the gun would burst, Sellmer ordered his men to move outside the battery before each shot fired.

A hairline crack developed in the Parrott rifle, a trait that was characteristic of the larger Parrott guns. Not wanting to slow the shelling, two lanyards were tied together on the gun. Finally, on the thirteenth shot of that evening, the thirty-sixth shot to be fired on Charleston from the Swamp Angel, the angel of death met her own demise. The gun's barrel could no longer contain the force of the 150-pound shell, and it burst, hurling itself off the gun carriage.

After the firing ceased, Vizetelly wrote:

> *It was now that, foiled at all points and smarting under his failures, the Federal general was guilty of that barbarity which has disgraced him as a soldier. Unable to capture the forts…he intimated that unless they were surrendered, he would turn his powerful guns upon the city. The threat was disregarded—disbelieved in, no doubt…in violation of warfare, he turned his guns on unoffending women and children.*

Though the short duration of the firing from the Swamp Angel did little to affect the Siege of Charleston, its accomplishments were far-reaching. The Swamp Angel firings were the first recorded firing of artillery shells using compass readings. The shells fired by the Parrott gun traveled farther

An engraving of the four-gun battery on Black Island, published in *Harper's Weekly*. *Author's collection*.

than any previous artillery fire in history. The construction of the marsh battery and the distance fired by the Swamp Angel were the most significant engineering accomplishments in the siege.

One Charlestonian observed, "The poorer class seek refuge on the race course and other open squares" in the upper city, out of range. The post office, banks, hospitals and many businesses moved their operations north of Calhoun Street. The children were evacuated at the Charleston Orphan House and taken to Orangeburg, South Carolina. Jacob Schirmer, a Charleston diarist, wrote, "Our prospects are darker and darker every day."

Gillmore, encouraged by the results of the Swamp Angel, ordered that a four-gun battery be placed nearby on Black Island, from which he continued to fire shells into Charleston.

Gillmore wrote to General Halleck in Washington, boasting, "The projectiles from my battery entered the city, and General Beauregard, himself designates them as 'the most destructive missiles ever used in war.'" There were no shells fired into Charleston in September 1863 and only a few in October. However, by the middle of November, the city of Charleston suffered regular bombardments.

8

"HELL CAN'T BE WORSE"

The late August bombardment of Fort Sumter by Union batteries on Morris Island was having a marked impact. Gillmore reported to General Halleck in Washington, "Fort Sumter is today a shapeless and harmless mass of ruins." He had fired more than five thousand shots against Fort Sumter to reduce the fort to rubble.

Dahlgren did not want to be left out, and he ordered five of his monitors to take up position eight hundred yards from Fort Sumter to attack. By this point, however, it was hard to have an effect firing on a fort that was little more than organized heaps of brick rubble and sand.

On September 1, six monitors assembled to attack Fort Sumter. They moved in single file with the *Weehawken* leading the way. At 11:30 a.m., when the monitors were within five hundred yards of Fort Sumter, the batteries on Sullivan's Island opened fire on the ships. Joined by the *New Ironsides*, the Union ships bombarded Fort Sumter for five hours, firing more than 240 shots and hitting the fort seventy-one times. The east wall of Fort Sumter suffered great damage. Some shells passed completely through the fort to hit the west wall. Fort Sumter's guns were no longer able to return the fire.

As the Union trenches were now dangerously close to Battery Wagner, Beauregard was fearful of losing his troops there and at Battery Gregg. The Confederate guns from the James Island batteries kept a constant fire on the advancing Union line. As the Union trench crews inched nearer, they faced many torpedoes and mines buried in the sand in front of Battery Wagner.

On September 4, 1863, Beauregard met with his general officers and his chief engineer, asking his staff a series of questions:

Battery B of the U.S. Artillery during the summer of 1863 siege on Battery Wagner. *Courtesy of the Library of Congress.*

Field artillery units are assembled on Morris Island in 1863 for an attack on Battery Wagner. *Courtesy of the Library of Congress.*

How long can Fort Wagner be held without regard for the safety of the garrison? How long can the battery be held with a "fair prospect of saving its garrison?" How long, after the loss or evacuation of Wagner, can Battery Gregg be held? Can the heavy guns at Batteries Wagner and Gregg be removed prior to evacuation without endangering the garrisons?

This Union naval battery on Morris Island used two eighty-pound Whitworth rifles to fire on Fort Sumter. *Courtesy of the Library of Congress.*

The Union headquarters of the field officer of the trenches on Morris Island. The zigzag trenches were used to slowly advance on formidable Battery Wagner. *Courtesy of the Library of Congress.*

Can we take the offensive, landing three thousand men on Morris Island, and attack the enemy?

After much discussion, the meeting was adjourned. The next day, Beauregard prepared a confidential order for the two garrisons to prepare for their simultaneous evacuation.

By September 5, the Federal flag, always flying on the most advanced trench, was only one hundred yards from Battery Wagner, abreast of the south angle of the battery.

On September 6, the Union army was close enough and ready to assault Battery Wagner for a third time. Edward W. Smith, assistant adjutant general for Gillmore, distributed Special Order No. 513, calling for the assault on Battery Wagner at 9:00 a.m. on September 7. The assault was planned utilizing three columns. The first column would attack the parapet of the seafront. The second column would charge the beach, pass the seafront of the fort and attack the north and west faces of Battery Wagner. The third column would follow the second column and deploy on the island in between Battery Wagner and Battery Gregg.

On the morning of September 6, Colonel L.M. Keitt, commander of Battery Wagner, sent an urgent dispatch to Beauregard:

> *The whole fort* [Wagner] *is weakened. A repetition tomorrow of today's firing will make the work almost a ruin. The* [Union] *mortar fire is still very heavy and fatal, and no important work can be done. Is it desirable to sacrifice the garrison? To continue to hold it* [Wagner] *is to do so.*

At 9:00 p.m. on the night of September 6, the Confederates began evacuating all of Morris Island. Captain T.A. Huguenin commanded a rear guard of thirty-five men to maintain watch as troops left Morris Island by boat. The evacuation by the nine hundred Confederate troops was complete by 1:30 a.m. During the evacuation, two boats with forty-seven men were captured by Union armed barges deployed between Cumming's Point and Fort Sumter.

The Confederates at Battery Wagner defiantly held their position for fifty-eight days, facing a Union army more than ten times their number supported by a fleet of armored vessels. From July 10 to September 7, facing two frontal assaults and the daily bombardment by Gillmore's batteries and the Union fleet, the total Confederate casualties numbered 641. The Union troops suffered casualties totaling 2,318 in the Morris Island campaign. In the same period, the Union army and navy fired more than sixty-two hundred rounds of artillery on Fort Sumter, but the Confederate garrison only suffered three men killed and forty-nine wounded.

After the capture of the two Confederate boats leaving the island, Gillmore was informed about the evacuation just after midnight. At 5:10

a.m. on September 7, Gillmore signaled to Dahlgren, "The whole island is ours, but the enemy have escaped us."

One soldier from a North Carolina regiment summed up his feeling about Battery Wagner after the evacuation:

> *I have heard preachers talk about Hell, a great big hole, full of fire and brimstone, where a bad fellow was dropped in, and I will allow it used to worry me at times, but Gentlemen, Hell can't be worse than Battery Wagner. I have got out of that, and the other place ain't going to worry me any more.*

9

"Must Be Held to the Bitter End"

B y the first of September, with no large guns operational, the fort was nothing more than an infantry outpost. Colonel Rhett was transferred to command the inner harbor fortifications, and Beauregard placed Major Stephen Elliott in command at Fort Sumter, notifying him:

> *You are to be sent to a fort deprived of all offensive capability, and having but one gun—a 32-pounder—with which to salute the flag, morning and evening. But that fort is Fort Sumter, the key to the entrance of this harbor. It must be held to the bitter end: not with artillery, as heretofore, but with infantry alone; and there can be no hope of reinforcements.*

Elliott received 320 fresh troops rotated to Fort Sumter. Knowing that Batteries Wagner and Gregg were being evacuated, Elliott recognized that he could face an amphibious assault on the fort. He requisitioned a supply of hand grenades and fireballs for his defense and placed wire and other obstructions at the tops of his crumbled walls to help thwart any attempt to cross over.

With morale high over the capture of Morris Island, on September 7, Dahlgren dispatched the *Weehawken* to mark the channel between Cumming's Point and Fort Sumter to make ready for a naval assault. While doing so, it ran aground. Dahlgren sent monitors to the area to distract the Confederates, but even at high tide, the captain could not dislodge the *Weehawken*. During the night, tugboats were sent in to free the ship but were not able to do so.

The next morning, the Confederates on James Island and at Fort Sumter realized the ship was stuck as it sat exposed at low tide. The Confederate

Major (illustrated here later as a brigadier general) Stephen Elliott, commander of Fort Sumter, September 1863 to May 1864. *Courtesy of Willis J. Keith.*

Union Battery Rosecrans, on Morris Island, used its three one-hundred-pound Parrott rifles to fire on Fort Sumter. *Courtesy of the Library of Congress.*

batteries opened fire trying to hit the underside of the ship from long range. Finally, in the afternoon, the *Weehawken* floated free and was able to withdraw.

Dahlgren sent a message to Elliott demanding the surrender Fort Sumter. Elliott simply responded, "Inform Admiral Dahlgren that he may have Fort Sumter when he can take it and hold it."

Accepting the challenge, Dahlgren planned an amphibious assault. He assigned Commander T.H. Stevens to lead the attack, telling him, "There is nothing but a corporal guard at the fort and all we have to do is go in and take it."

The relationship between the Union army and navy was never a great one, as jealousies and egos collided, and by September 1863, the relationship between Gillmore and Dahlgren was at a breaking point. Both Gillmore and Dahlgren wanted the honor of taking Fort Sumter, perhaps the greatest prize of the war, but Gillmore insisted that any collaboration between the army and navy be under army command. Dahlgren refused, and Gillmore withdrew his support for a joint operation and planned his own assault.

On the afternoon of September 8, the Confederate ironclad *Chicora* intercepted Union messages that an amphibious assault would occur that

Rear Admiral Dahlgren's signalmen aboard the USS *Pawnee*. *Courtesy of the Library of Congress.*

night. Unknown to the Union navy, when the Confederates salvaged the guns from the USS *Keokuk*, they also recovered a Union codebook. Elliott was now ready for the defense of the island rubble—Fort Sumter.

That night, five hundred Union sailors and marines boarded small boats and were towed by the tugboat *Daffodil* to within four hundred yards of Fort Sumter. From there they rowed to the fort for the assault, unaware that Elliott and three hundred troops from the Charleston Battalion watched them from the fort. As the Union assault neared the southeastern and southern faces of the fort, they were expecting nothing more than token resistance.

Elliott ordered his men to hold fire until the Union force was within yards of the fort. They then greeted the sailors and marines with a barrage of musket fire, hand grenades, brickbats and fireballs. The Confederate gunboat *Chicora*, positioned nearby, opened fire on the Union attackers with canister and grapeshot, as did the guns at Fort Moultrie and Fort Johnson.

Taking on intense fire, the supporting Union ships withdrew, abandoning the sailors and marines on the rocks at the fort. That night, 124 of Dahlgren's men were killed, wounded or captured, and four boats were lost. Gillmore's men never arrived at Fort Sumter. The low tide on the night of the eighth kept them detained at Morris Island. Clearly, both Dahlgren and Gillmore had miscalculated the ability and determination of the small Confederate garrison at Fort Sumter.

After the failed amphibious assault, the relationship between Dahlgren and Gillmore continued to deteriorate. Dahlgren had earlier requested support from the army batteries on Morris Island as he considered any further attack on Fort Sumter. Gillmore responded sarcastically. Dahlgren wrote to Gillmore on September 29 that his purpose was "merely to ask the only co-operation that you can afford me, after having for sixty days yielded cheerfully to every request made of me." Dahlgren ended the letter with his own sarcasm, saying, "I regret to occupy your time and mine with these remarks."

Gillmore, in his return letter two days later, acquiesced to Dahlgren's point. He offered:

> *These operations have all had direct reference to the immediate end in view, the passage of the ironclads into the inner harbor. Every shot I have fired, and every foot of trench that I have dug, have looked to that result.*

He ended the letter, offering, "What I stipulate for is a continuance of that cordial, open, and sincere exchange of views that has characterized our efforts thus far."

After the capture of Morris Island, Gillmore was premature in a declaration to his troops in which he announced:

> *Fort Sumter is destroyed. The scene where our country's flag suffered its first dishonor you made the theater of one of its proudest moments.*

The Union telegraph bombproof on Morris Island. *Courtesy of the Library of Congress.*

The fort has been in the possession of the enemy for more than two years; has been his pride and boast; has been strengthened by every appliance known to military science, and has defied the assaults of the most powerful and gallant fleet the world ever saw; but it has yielded to your courage and patient labor. Its walls are now crumbled to ruins, its formidable batteries are silenced, and, though a hostile flag still floats over it, the fort is a harmless and helpless wreck.

Throughout the rest of September, Gillmore's batteries on Morris Island and Dahlgren's gunboats paid little attention to Fort Sumter. Dahlgren was hesitant to plan another ironclad attack knowing that the firepower at Fort Moultrie had been increased. Gillmore concentrated on rebuilding and arming the captured Confederate positions at Battery Wagner and Battery Gregg. By the end of September 1863, Gillmore accumulated twenty-two hundred troops on Morris, Folly and Kiawah Islands.

After the capture of Morris Island, Gillmore was promoted to major general. Battery Wagner was renamed Fort Strong, in honor of Union brigadier general George Strong who died of his injuries on the July 18 assault on the battery. Battery Gregg was renamed Fort Putnam, in honor of brigade commander Colonel Haldiman Putnam, killed in the same attack.

In October 1863, the garrison at Fort Sumter began remounting some of its guns. On October 26, Gillmore opened fire on Fort Sumter from Forts Strong and Putnam. Dahlgren supported the attack with fire from the

Fort Sumter after the intense Union bombardment. *Courtesy of the Collection of the US House of Representatives.*

The interior of Union Fort Putnam, formerly Battery Gregg. *Courtesy of the Library of Congress.*

An interior view of Fort Strong on Morris Island, formerly Battery Wagner. *Courtesy of the Library of Congress.*

Patapsco and *Lehigh*. This action began the second great bombardment of Fort Sumter, which would last for forty-one days.

One soldier wrote of daily life in the fort during this time:

> *All that we can see is the bursting of shells, and the flying of bricks, and fragments of shells through the air, and our sole thought is how to keep out of the way of them. The continued cry of the sentinels "Look out" from the parapet continuously in the ear, until every sound seems to bear the same refrain. On yesterday one of the sentinels on post was literally torn into pieces by a shell. Poor fellow he never knew what hurt him!*

Most of the top of Fort Sumter's walls and the gorge wall were reduced. Major Elliott grew concerned that another amphibious assault may be attempted as the debris fell outward from the fort, leaving the fort vulnerable to a breach. Theodore Honour, a private with the Washington Light Infantry stationed at Fort Sumter, recorded in his journal:

> *The sea-face to the fort is completely demolished, and in its stead is an incline of rubbish that will make it no difficult matter for the Yanks to land, and try by a desperate charge to fain entrance to the fort, but we are here to defend that weak spot.*

The bombardment of Fort Sumter lasted into December as sometimes more than one thousand artillery rounds were fired each day onto the fort. With no large guns left in Fort Sumter capable of responding, the Confederate batteries on James and Sullivan's Islands fired on the Morris Island Federal positions. During this period, the Confederate troops in Fort Sumter never numbered more than three hundred. A Confederate ironclad and rowboats staged at Fort Johnson and Sullivan's Island were ready to help defend against any attempt at another amphibious assault.

While the Parrott rifled guns were favored by Union artillerymen, they were noted for bursting from constant and repetitive use. Most Parrotts would only last for several hundred shots. Occasionally, a gun might last for 1,000 shots, but that was rare. One thirty-pound Parrott rifle mounted by the Union army at Cummings Point performed remarkably. In a period of sixty-nine days, the gun fired 4,594 rounds on Charleston before it burst.

On November 2, Jefferson Davis made a visit to Charleston, arriving by train. He was met at the depot by Beauregard and members of the city council. The strained relationship between Beauregard and Davis was still evident in the president's speech given at city hall. Davis made no mention of the accomplishments by Beauregard and the general officers in thus far thwarting the Union siege. The only officer Davis recognized was Elliott, commanding the garrison at Fort Sumter. Davis did close his speech with a prayer "for the sacred soil of Charleston."

After the festivities in the city, Beauregard and General Hagood escorted Davis on a horse ride across James Island. Hagood noted, "Mr. Davis inspected the works closely, going at a rapid gallop with his cortege from battery to battery and stopping long enough to receive a salute." That evening, former Governor Aiken hosted a gala in honor of the Confederate president.

At 3:00 a.m. on November 30, 250 Union troops on barges were spotted approaching Fort Sumter. The garrison opened fire once the invaders were within three hundred yards. After the guns at Sullivan's Island and Fort Johnson also opened fire, the barges withdrew.

Finally, on December 6, after firing more than eighteen thousand shots on the battered fort, the daily bombardment on Fort Sumter subsided. Engineers began making some minor improvements to the fort. Gabions, wicker baskets filled with sand, were placed on the crumbling walls of the fort. A three-gun battery was mounted on the northeast face of Fort Sumter, designed to keep any Union ship from making a run to the inner harbor. A 275-foot underground tunnel was built to allow movement through the fort under protective cover.

The Union gunners turned their attention to the city of Charleston, firing regularly. The gunners sighted on the steeple at St. Michael's Church. The

The breach on the north wall at Fort Sumter is patched with gabions, wicker baskets filled with sand. *Courtesy of the Library of Congress.*

church was hit frequently, leaving the interior, the chancel and the organ heavily damaged. One Charlestonian wrote:

> *Poor dear old Charleston! I hear the desolation in the lower part of the town is appalling. Lately the shells have done a good deal of damage, altho' the papers properly make no reference to it. Twice they have come very near St. Michael's spire—the City Hall, Court House, Guard House have all been struck.*

Even the sacred passing of Christmas was not safe from the Union artillery. Just after midnight on the holy day, the Union guns opened fire on Charleston with the greatest intensity yet. Shells started a fire on Broad Street that quickly began to spread. Shortly, another fire broke out at the corner of Church Street and St. Michael's Alley. The city's firemen fought the fires with their usual determination, though the Union shells continued to rain around them.

A Confederate soldier on James Island could see the bombardment and wrote, "The Yankees as soon as they saw the sight of the fire poured their shells like rain around the neighborhood of the fire." Beauregard, in his report to Adjutant General Cooper, noted, "Six houses burned by fire of yesterday [Christmas] and 7 persons wounded by it and enemy's firing on city. He threw 150 shells, of which 19 fell short."

10

"Cigar Steamer for Carrying Spar Torpedoes"

Even as the Confederate ironclads *Chicora* and *Palmetto State* were under construction, Beauregard expressed his preference for a "torpedo ram" designed by Captain Francis D. Lee. Lee's design utilized a torpedo as the primary weapon, as opposed to the large guns planned for the ironclad gunboats. Though it was too late to stop construction of the first two gunboats, Beauregard urged Mallory to suspend plans for a third ironclad and divert the funds and materials to Lee's ram.

Lee designed a long, narrow ironclad ship that sat low in the water. Attached to the front of the ram would be a spar torpedo that could be lowered to hit an enemy ship below the waterline. This would expose even the Union ironclads and monitors to effective attack since they had less armor below the waterline.

In a letter to Governor Pickens on October 8, 1862, Beauregard informed him:

> Captain F.D. Lee submitted to me yesterday a plan for a "torpedo ram," which I believe would be worth several gunboats. I can only express my regret that it was not adopted at once by the naval department at Richmond when submitted to it several months ago, as he informs me. I fear not to put on record now that half a dozen of these "torpedo rams," of small comparative cost, would keep this harbor clear of four times the number of the enemy's ironclad gunboats.

Four days later, Beauregard wrote to Mr. J.K. Sass, chairman of the South Carolina State Committee on Gunboats:

I have the honor to request that the materials being collected for the State's new gun boat should be applied to the Torpedo Ram, which, I am informed, can be got ready much sooner (in less than 2 months), will cost less, probably not over $100,000, and will be more efficient, in my opinion. In other words, I think the State and the Country would be the gainers by constructing these new Engines of destruction in place of the intended gun boat now just commencing to be built.

Though he was not successful in convincing the state or the Confederate government to proceed with Lee's ram over the ironclad gunboats, Beauregard was not deterred. Again, in writing to Pickens on November 8, the general argued that the ironclad gunboats would "effect but little against the enemy's new gigantic monitors." Beauregard implored, "We must attack them under water, where they are the most vulnerable, if we wish to destroy them, and the torpedo ram is the only probable way of accomplishing that desirable end."

In December, Beauregard ordered Lee to purchase a local steamer and salvage its engines and iron for use in building a torpedo ram. Despite this salvage, they could not obtain enough materials to build the ram. In a report, Beauregard protested, "I find so much difficulty in procuring mechanics and materials here for the construction of Captain Lee's torpedo ram that I will have to stop its construction."

Though impressed with the January 1863 attacks of the *Chicora* and *Palmetto State*, he understood that their slow speed kept a naval victory from becoming a complete success. He also realized that the Confederate gunboats had not yet faced the new Union monitors, a more formidable enemy than the wooden warships.

By March 1863, construction on Lee's ram had halted. Instead, using materials that could be obtained, they built a wooden, hand-powered ram. In March 1863, William T. Glassel, an officer on the *Chicora*, commanded the wooden ram, rowed by a seven-man crew, in an attack against the USS *Powhatan*, a wooden steam frigate participating in the blockade. A lookout spotted the ram, and one of Glassel's crewmen panicked and rowed against the others. As the tide began pulling the ram, and with the element of surprise lost, Glassel broke off the attack. After this failed attack, the idea of hand-cranked rams was abolished.

Another attempt by Lee at creating a ram resulted in the CSS *Torch*. This ship was similar to the *Chicora* and *Palmetto State*, though much smaller at twenty feet in length. Instead of being armed with guns, it carried three one-hundred-pound torpedoes mounted on poles on the front of the ship. Unlike the hand-cranked ram, the *Torch* was powered by a steam engine. A steam engine was salvaged from the tugboat *Barton* and refurbished by Cameron & Company in Charleston.

Still, Lee could not get the armor to complete the *Torch*, so he used granite as ballast to lower the ship in the water. By August 1, the steam-powered ram was complete, less armor, and successfully completed its trials. Captain James Carlin, an experienced blockade runner from the *Ella and Annie*, was selected to command the ram.

On August 20, steaming through the harbor, Carlin stopped at Fort Sumter and picked up Lieutenant E.S. Fickling and eleven soldiers from the First South Carolina Artillery to serve as sharpshooters. After midnight, Carlin set his sights on the USS *New Ironsides*. A Union officer noted "a strange vessel, sitting low in the water and having the appearance of being a large boat, coming up astern very fast." After being hailed, Carlin answered that he was "the steamer *Live Yankee*," a Union ship from Port Royal.

Carlin lowered his torpedo boom for attack, though he was now parallel to his target. He ordered a right turn, but his helmsman was slow in turning the ship. The anxious sharpshooters aboard the *Torch* almost fired a volley, but Carlin called them off. The captain of the *New Ironsides* slipped the chain of his anchor to allow quick movement. While backing astern, the Union ironclad fired its bow guns at the *Torch*.

The *Torch* did escape the guns of the *New Ironsides* but did not complete its own attack. Carlin was displeased with the ability of the ship, noting it was his "duty most unhesitatingly to express my condemnation of the vessel and engine for the purposes it was intended." He suggested the Confederacy make "a transport out of her."

The Confederate government offered a bounty equal to 50 percent of the value of any Union blockading ship destroyed. Additionally, Theodore D. Wagner of John Fraser & Company in Charleston offered a bounty of $100,000 in gold to anyone who could sink the *New Ironsides*, $50,000 for sinking a Union monitor and $25,000 for sinking a wooden warship.

In the summer of 1863, another type of torpedo boat was under construction. South Carolinian Theodore D. Stoney invested $25,000 to start the Southern Torpedo Company. He was joined by Theodore Wagner and others who invested as well. Utilizing a design prototype by Ross Winan of Baltimore, Dr. St. Julien Ravenel designed a small torpedo steamer. The boat was constructed at Stony Landing on the upper Cooper River, thirty miles from Charleston.

The torpedo boat was only fifty-four feet long and less than six feet wide. Lee described the boat as a "cigar steamer for carrying spar torpedoes." David C. Ebaugh of Maryland was the head mechanic for the project. He was assisted by John Chaulk and Samuel Easterby. Dr. Ravenel supervised the construction. The torpedo boat was named *David*. Ebaugh claimed it was named for him; however, it was Ravenel's wife who suggested the biblical name David, given that the small boat would face the "Goliaths" of the Union navy.

Stoney wrote to Beauregard about the formation of the Southern Torpedo Company, asking that he sanction the project. Beauregard responded, "I will be most happy to afford the company all the facilities in my power for carrying into effect their proposed plans and operations, and may fortune smile on their patriotic efforts."

After completion, the *David* was transferred to the Atlantic Wharf at the end of Broad Street. Lieutenant Glassel was select to command the new torpedo boat. James W. Tomb, assistant engineer; J. Walker Cannon, pilot; and James Stuart, fireman, served as the crew. They completed a series of successful trials in the inner harbor recording speeds between six and seven knots.

After nightfall on October 5, 1863, Glassel took the *David* to confront the *New Ironsides*. Each member of the crew was armed with both a revolver and a shotgun. Though the *David* sat low in the water, a lookout on the

This *Harper's Weekly* engraving depicts the Confederate torpedo boat *David* steaming toward the USS *New Ironsides* on October 5, 1863. *Author's collection.*

"Cigar Steamer for Carrying Spar Torpedoes"

A *Harper's Weekly* engraving, published in 1863, of the *David*'s torpedo exploding at the USS *New Ironsides*, damaging but not sinking the ironclad ship. *Author's collection.*

New Ironsides spotted the torpedo boat when it was three hundred yards out. Hailing the boat but receiving no response, the Union sailors opened fire with small arms.

Now only forty yards away and moving quickly, Glassel fired his shotgun, wounding the Union officer on the watch. He rammed his torpedo into the side of the Union ship. The resulting explosion disabled the *David*'s engine and left a hole in the side of the *New Ironsides*. Without power, Glassel ordered his crew to scuttle the *David* and abandon ship. As Glassel, Tomb and Stuart jumped overboard, Cannon stayed on the ship since he could not swim. The *David* drifted clear of the *New Ironsides*, and Tomb swam back to join Cannon on the ship. They were finally able to restart the steam engine and return to Charleston.

Sullivan was captured as he held onto the rudder chain of the *New Ironsides*. Glassel was struggling, trying to swim to Fort Sumter, and was captured by a Union boat. They were both taken prisoner and held aboard the USS *Ottawa*, a wooden gunboat. They were later taken to New York to be tried for "using an engine of war not recognized by civilized nations." Instead, they were transferred to Union prisons in the North until they were exchanged for the captain and a crewman from the captured USS *Isaac P. Smith*. The *David* carried out missions through 1864 in the Stono and North Edisto Rivers and on the blockade fleet in the harbor, though none was as successful as the attack on the *New Ironsides*.

In January 1864, the Southern Torpedo Company notified Beauregard that it expected "two more steamers afloat tomorrow or next day." Dahlgren was impressed with the *David* class of torpedo boats and urged the U.S. Navy to construct its own steamers on a similar design. He also encouraged the Federal government to establish a bounty for any *David* captured or destroyed. In April 1864, Confederate secretary of the navy Stephen Russell Mallory wrote to Commander Bullock, a Confederate representative in England, to secure "twelve small marine engines and boiler" to construct torpedo boats.

After the *New Ironsides* was repaired, calcium lights were transferred from the army on Morris Island to light around the ship at night to prevent a repeat torpedo attack. They also used tugboats to patrol around the ships at anchor in the blockade fleet. Though other torpedo boats were constructed, they were ineffective since they relied on the element of surprise.

11

"WONDERFUL FISH-SHAPED BOAT"

In early 1864, the firing on Fort Sumter was intermittent, but the bombardment of Charleston continued in earnest. In January, for a period of nine days, more than fifteen hundred rounds were fired into the city. Realizing that most of lower Charleston was already devastated, the Union gunners shifted their aim from the St. Michael's steeple to that of St. Philip's Church, forcing the congregation to move their worship to St. Paul's Church, north of Calhoun Street.

The *Charleston Daily Courier*, in January 1864, reported on one instance when a "shell passed through a bed containing three children and exploded in the next floor." The article observed that the fact that "no one was injured is regarded as miraculous." A Northern newspaper concluded, "Block by block of that city is being reduced to ashes, and by a process as steadily inexorable as that which Gillmore humbled Pulaski and Sumter."

In February 1864, Confederate innovation would be responsible for another incredible feat in the defense of Charleston. Inventors Horace L. Hunley, James McClintock and Baxter Watson developed a submarine in New Orleans. The *Pioneer* was successfully tested in February 1862 in the Mississippi River. When Union forces advanced on New Orleans, the submersible ship was scuttled to prevent its capture.

Hunley, McClintock and Watson moved to Mobile, Alabama, and developed a second submarine, named the *American Diver*. It made one unsuccessful attack in February 1863 and later sank in Mobile Bay after a storm.

After the loss of the *American Diver*, construction began on a third submarine. People referred to the submersible oddity as the "fish boat," the "fish torpedo boat" or the "porpoise." The submarine, named *H.L. Hunley*, was designed to hold a crew of eight who would propel the ship by a hand-cranked propeller.

The *Hunley* was successfully tested in Mobile Bay in July 1863 and shipped to Charleston by rail in August. Susan Middleton, writing to her cousin Harriott, described the Hunley:

> *You will have heard, of course of the wonderful fish-shaped boat, built at Mobile, and brought here in sections overland. It goes entirely under water, has a propeller at one end, and torpedo at the other. It has fins, with valves in them to let in air—altho' it holds a sufficient supply to last 8 men 3 hours after it is submerged. Papa has seen a man, who saw a man, who made a voyage in this contrivance from one wharf to another—he was 20 minutes under water—and suffered no inconvenience. The inventor tells Mr. Read he is sure the boat will do its part, and if he had not been confident that his heart would not fail him he would never have come so far to make the attempt.*

Lieutenant John A. Payne, of the CSS *Chicora*, volunteered to command the *Hunley*, and crew members from both the *Chicora* and *Palmetto State* volunteered to serve on the submarine. On August 29, 1863, as the crew was preparing to test and train on the submarine, Payne stepped on a lever, causing the *Hunley* to dive underwater. Unfortunately, the hatches were still open, flooding the submarine and drowning five of the crew.

Susan Middleton, again in writing to her cousin, reported the second mishap with the fish-boat:

> *Eight more men have been drowned in the diving-boat. They were experimenting with her. Went down safely and rose under a vessel in the harbor—tapped on her bottom to show they were there—but, the next time they dive[d], something went wrong and she filled.*

The *Hunley* sank, drowning all of its crew, including Horace L. Hunley.

The USS *Housatonic* was responsible for the capture of the British blockade runner *Princess Royal* in January 1863, capturing what was called "the war's most important single cargo of contraband." In the following year, the *Housatonic* continued to capture many blockade runners attempting to slip into Charleston Harbor.

In February 1864, the 1,240-ton sloop, long a thorn in the side of Charleston blockade runners, was still patrolling as part of the blockading

The USS *Housatonic. Courtesy of the U.S. Navy Historical Center.*

fleet. On February 19, the *Housatonic*, commanded by Charles Pickering, was on duty just outside the Charleston bar. The officer of the deck sighted an object in the water just one hundred yards off, reporting that "it had the appearance of a plank moving in the water." He sounded the alarm, and all hands were called to quarters, but within two minutes, the *Hunley* rammed its spar torpedo into the starboard side of the Union ship.

The explosion quickly sank the *Housatonic*. Two officers and three men were killed in the attack. The *Hunley* survived the attack but sank approximately an hour later. Confederate lieutenant colonel O.M. Dantzler at Battery Marshall on Sullivan's Island reported seeing the blue light signal, indicating the *Hunley* was returning. The exact cause for the sinking of the *Hunley* is unknown.

Union reports indicated that the "sloop-of-war *Housatonic* [was] destroyed by a torpedo off Morris Island." With the submarine missing, Beauregard announced the following day, "As soon as its fate shall have been ascertained [we will] pay a proper tribute to the gallantry and patriotism of its crew and officers."

On February 21, Beauregard reported to Richmond:

> *A gun-boat* [Housatonic] *sunken off Battery Marshall. Supposed to have been done by Mobile torpedo-boat, under Lieut. George E. Dixon,*

Company E, Twenty-first Alabama Volunteers, which went out for that purpose, and which, I regret to say, has not been heard of since.

In March 1864, Beauregard received word that his wife, Caroline Deslonde Beauregard, living in Union-occupied New Orleans, had died. She had suffered an illness since the fall of New Orleans. Union major general Nathaniel Banks graciously provided a steamer to transport Mrs. Beauregard's body upriver to her native St. James Parish for burial, where more than six thousand people attended her funeral. Beauregard wrote that he would like to rescue "her hallowed grave" from Union-occupied Louisiana.

The Union bombardment of Charleston continued through the spring. On one occasion in May 1864, Union shells started a fire at the corner of Elliott Street and Gadsden Alley. After the firemen arrived, Charleston diarist Schirmer noted, "The engine of the Phoenix Company was struck by a shell and blown to atoms." Emma Holmes in Charleston wrote, "Dear old Charleston still receives her allotted portion of battering, and 'The Gillmore District' is showing ghastly rents in many a once fair and goodly mansion."

Confederate major Edward Manigault wrote of a trip to the "lower part of the city":

From the "Bend" of King Street, fennel, weeds and grass growing in gutters. Broad Street has the pavement clear for the breadth of a single carriage way; all the rest grown up in grass with weeds and fennel, some of the fennel more than 6 feet high. The cows are actually grazing in the lower part of Meeting and Church Streets.

On May 1, 1864, Gillmore and eighteen thousand troops departed Charleston for Fort Monroe on the Virginia peninsula. Dahlgren's fleet was also reduced as some of the gunboats and the man-of-war *New Ironsides* departed for duty northward.

Later in May, Confederate captain John C. Mitchel relieved Elliott of command at Fort Sumter. Mitchel was the son of the famous Irish nationalist John Mitchel, who escaped to America and became publisher of the *Southern Citizen*.

By spring 1864, both armies in Charleston had new commanding officers. Beauregard was called to Richmond to assist Robert E. Lee with the defense of Richmond. He was replaced by Major General Samuel Jones. Jones had commanded the Army of Western Virginia from December 1862 to March 1864.

Captain John C. Mitchel, commander of Fort Sumter, was mortally wounded by a shell fragment on July 20, 1864. *Courtesy of Willis J. Keith.*

Confederate major Samuel Jones. *Courtesy of the Library of Congress.*

Major General John G. Foster replaced Gillmore in Charleston. Foster was an engineer in Robert Anderson's command at Fort Sumter in 1861. The anger over the forced evacuation of their post by Beauregard was a memory that left Foster highly motivated to accomplish what Gillmore could not—the surrender of Fort Sumter and the capture of Charleston. Foster exclaimed, "To capture Richmond would be grand, but to capture Charleston would be glorious."

In late June, Foster launched a five-pronged attack on Charleston. A force was sent to sever the Charleston and Savannah Railroad at White Point on the North Edisto River. Brigadier General Alexander Schimmelfennig would land a force on James Island, and a second group would launch an amphibious assault on Fort Johnson. Five thousand Union troops would cross John's Island to attack the upper Stono River. The gunboats would bombard the Confederate batteries on southwest James Island. And Fort Sumter would be bombarded.

Knowing that thirteen warships and forty-six transports departed Port Royal, the Confederates were expecting an attack. On the morning of July 2, twenty-five hundred Union troops landed on southern James Island. Though they had some initial success, Confederate forces counterattacked, forcing the Union troops back to the Stono River.

At 2:00 a.m. on July 3, 1,000 Union troops departed Morris Island to make an amphibious attack near Fort Johnson. This mission was a disaster as 119 Union troops were killed or wounded. Confederate lieutenant colonel Yates captured more prisoners than he had men.

The Union gunboats attacked Battery Pringle on the Stono River. Though they bombarded the Confederate position for days, Battery Pringle was not silenced. The same day, Brigadier General John P. Hatch landed on Seabrook Island with four thousand troops to cross John's Island. After two days of skirmishes on John's Island, Hatch withdrew.

Union general David Bell Birney moved up the North Edisto River, accompanied by three gunboats. He landed unopposed at White Point but found himself in a fight later with a Confederate battery at King's Creek. The gunboats moved up the Dawhoo River to shell the Confederate battery but fired on their own troops by mistake. After two hours with no success, Birney's troops were pulled to reinforce Schimmelfennig on James Island.

By July 11, the Union attacks subsided with no real accomplishment. Dahlgren met with Foster and Hatch on John's Island. Foster declared that "he had done all he intended." Dahlgren would later write, "I am utterly disgusted." Another Union officer wrote, "The combined movements,

"Wonderful Fish-Shaped Boat"

A Federal mortar battery with crew on Morris Island. *Courtesy of the Library of Congress.*

admirably planned, against a weaker enemy came to naught, for want of concerted action and persistence in attack. At every point we largely outnumbered the enemy."

On July 7, 1864, at first light, the bombardment of Fort Sumter resumed. Union batteries fired an average of 350 rounds a day as portions of the fort's wall were knocked down but accomplished little more than contributing to the enormous piles of debris. As the shelling relented each night, the Confederate troops and workmen continued to place wire fencing and other entanglements on top of the rubble to discourage an amphibious assault. Union batteries tried to interfere with the nightly work by firing mortar rounds on the fort.

Confederate engineer Captain John Johnson requisitioned one thousand bags of sand to be delivered to Fort Sumter each night. The sand bags, with the masonry debris, were effective in absorbing the concussion of the Union shells, actually making Fort Sumter stronger.

The channel side of Fort Sumter is reinforced with palmetto logs. *Courtesy of the Library of Congress.*

A powder monkey aboard the USS *New Hampshire*, a Union supply ship servicing the blockading ships. *Courtesy of the Library of Congress.*

A Boston newspaper proclaimed, "It is a military axiom that every fortified place can be taken, *if* only proper means are expended. The Government means that there shall be no failure in the *if* in this case." However, by late July, Dahlgren felt that Fort Sumter was "nearly impregnable."

On the afternoon of July 20, Captain Mitchel climbed the western wall of the fort with his spyglass to note the position of the Federal ships for his daily report. A mortar shell from Morris Island burst overhead, and a shell fragment tore into his hip. Mitchel died of his wounds four hours later. Legend holds that his last words were, "I willingly give my life for South Carolina. Oh, that I could have died for Ireland." After Mitchel's death, Captain Thomas A. Huguenin was placed in command.

The firing slowed in August as Foster's supply of ammunition was running low. Finally, in early September, the bombardment that had started sixty days earlier stopped. More than 14,666 rounds were fired onto Fort Sumter but with the same result as before. The situation in Charleston seemed to have reached a stalemate. Though firing would continue sporadically, this ended the last great bombardment of Fort Sumter.

12

"Its Inhumane Threat"

B y the summer of 1863, the Federal government had ceased paroles and prisoner exchanges, feeling it was "preferable to feed prisoners than to fight soldiers." Of course, this policy left thousands of Union prisoners in Southern prisons under deplorable conditions. This accomplished the desired objective—the South was becoming overwhelmed with Union prisoners, requiring troops to guard them and food to feed them with both commodities in short supply.

On June 13, 1864, Major General Jones informed Foster that five Union generals and forty-five field officers "have been sent to this city [Charleston] for safe-keeping." The letter noted that the prisoners would be placed in an area of the city occupied by noncombatants. In concluding, Jones pointed out, "It is proper, however, that I should inform you that it is a part of the city which has been for many months exposed day and night to the fire of your guns." The Union officers were placed in the home of Colonel James O'Connor at 180 Broad Street.

Foster, predictably, was incensed. He forwarded Jones's letter to Lincoln and requested that fifty Confederate officers be transferred to Morris Island and placed within range of the Confederate shelling on those positions. Upon hearing this, the five Union generals held in Charleston wrote to Foster:

> *The journals of this morning inform us, for the first time, that five general officers of the Confederate service have arrived at Hilton Head, with a view to their being subjected to the same treatment that we are receiving here. We think it just to ask for these officers every kindness and courtesy that you*

A Union officer held prisoner in Charleston sketched this scene of Broad Street in 1865, published in *Harper's Weekly. Author's collection.*

can extend to them in acknowledgement of the fact that we, at this time, are as pleasantly and comfortably situated as is possible for prisoners of war, receiving from the Confederate authorities every privilege that we could desire or expect, nor are we unnecessarily exposed to fire.

Suddenly, and despite the prevailing policy, after three weeks Foster agreed to exchange fifty Confederate officers for the fifty Union officers held in Charleston. Confederate brigadier general Basil Duke, one of the prisoners, wrote of the exchange:

After the customary formalities had been gone through with and the exchange completed, a banquet was given the prisoners on both sides, in which the officers conducting the exchange and some of the officers of the fleet participated. To the Confederates and doubtless to the others so long accustomed to prison fare, this feast seemed ambrosial, almost incredible… in honor of the occasion, the big guns on both sides boomed out thunderous salutes when the exchange was concluded.

In 1864, the Confederate prison at Andersonville was receiving more than 400 Union prisoners a day. By August 1864, the prison was filled to capacity, with 32,899 prisoners. Andersonville prisoners were dying at an alarming rate due to the crowded conditions, poor food and inadequate medical care, and more captured soldiers continued to arrive. The Confederacy appealed to the Federal government to reinstate the exchange policy. Hoping to convince the Union secretary of war, a number of Andersonville prisoners were paroled and sent to Washington.

Edward W. Boate of the Forty-second New York Infantry chaired a delegation of six prisoners sent to Washington. On the way, the delegation was taken to Prison Oglethorpe in Macon, Georgia, where Union officers were held. One Union general, an inmate there, presented the delegation with a letter for President Lincoln in which he urged an exchange "not for officers he said, but for the brave men who had fought so gallantly in the field, and suffered so much in prison." When the prisoner delegation finally reached Washington, Lincoln declined to see them.

In an effort to alleviate the overcrowding at Andersonville, a new prison, Camp Lawton, was established seventy-five miles away at Millen, northwest of Savannah. Prisoners were also sent to Savannah and Charleston in an effort to further reduce the population at Andersonville. By September 1864, only five thousand prisoners remained at Andersonville, but already more than ten thousand had died.

The Charleston Workhouse, as seen in this *Harper's Weekly* engraving, was used as an overflow site to hold Union prisoners. Captain H.A. Coats of the Eighty-fifth New York wrote of his experience there: "There was but one privy, never cleaned out…Later, enlisted men were brought and filled the jail to overflowing." *Author's collection.*

Many Union prisoners were confined at the Charleston Jail on Magazine Street, seen in this *Harper's Weekly* engraving. The ground floor held civil convicts; the second floor held Confederate officers under punishment; the third floor held Negro prisoners; and the fourth floor held Union and Confederate deserters. Union prisoners were also detained in the walled jail yard. *Author's collection.*

Jones vehemently protested the movement of prisoners to Charleston but was overruled by superiors. Several hundred Union prisoners were placed at the O'Connor House; on the grounds of the Charleston Jail and Workhouse and Roper Hospital; and at the racecourse, north of the city. The numbers of prisoners at Charleston quickly increased.

Lieutenant Louis R. Fortescue, U.S. Signal Corps, wrote of his incarceration:

> *Our quarters here are the worst kind imaginable, 600 officers packed into a small prison yard, not more than 100 yards square with walls surrounding us at least 20 feet high and not a single shade tree…Transferred this evening to the Marion Hospital a large building adjoining the Prison. It is quite commodious and are really the best quarters I have had the pleasure of enjoying since my advent into the Confederacy.*

Jones wrote to Confederate secretary of war James Seddon, pleading, "Please have the order revoked or send me additional troops. It is with great difficulty that these now here can be guarded; no others can be at present." Jones was also well aware that additional prisoners placed in the city would, once again, raise the ire of Foster. However, Seddon had no choice in the matter. The Confederacy was fighting a war on four fronts by mid-1864, and with the Federal government still refusing to exchange prisoners, it had few options.

Though Foster handled himself with Jones much differently, in writing to General Halleck in Washington he conceded the challenges facing Jones and the Confederacy:

> The truth is they are so short of men as guards they have no place to put their prisoners except in Savannah and Charleston…As far as injury goes to them there can be none, for I know their exact location and direct the shells accordingly.

Foster offered to Halleck that Jones was "very desirous to have an exchange effected…I can easily have the matter arranged." Following the established policy, Halleck did not instruct Foster to make any exchanges.

In his communications with Jones, Foster insisted that there would be retaliation for the Union prisoners brought to Charleston. In a dispatch on August 15, Foster notified Jones that "600 Confederate officers, prisoners of war, are to be sent here to be placed under the fire of your guns." He had the audacity to inquire as to the exact number of Union officers held in Charleston so he could adjust his number accordingly.

On the morning of August 20, 1864, six hundred Confederate officers held at the Fort Delaware prison were ordered to prepare for relocation. They packed their few ragtag possessions, mostly clothes and tattered blankets. Some officers were fortunate to have books; others retained their sabers, as was the custom for officers held prisoner. That afternoon, the officers, including fifty who were wounded, marched in columns of four to the prison gate and boarded the *Crescent City*, a side-wheel steamship.

Captain John J. Dunkle, Twenty-fifth Virginia Infantry, wrote of the voyage:

> About three-fourths of us became very sick shortly after leaving Fort Delaware. We contracted sea-sickness not being familiar with the sea and sea voyages. And as closely confined as we were, the spectacle was horrid—the entire floor was covered with sick men—horribly sick, vomited to a fearful extent by the disease, and groaning in a terrific manner…Even those of us who were not infected by the sickening malady, were made faint by the loathsome spectacle we were obliged to witness.

The ship arrived in Port Royal and then proceeded to Charleston, arriving on August 29. On September 1, the *Crescent City* made anchor near Fort Strong at Morris Island. The prisoners could see the shelling of Charleston through the portholes on the ship.

On September 4, Foster wrote to Jones:

> *I demanded the removal from under our fire of any prisoners of war who might be held by you in confinement at Charleston…you admit that you still retain prisoners of war at that point, where they are exposed to fire…I have therefore to inform you that your officers, now in my hands, will be placed by me under your fire, as an act of retaliation.*

Jones immediately responded and reminded Foster that the prisoners were only in Charleston temporarily, though he did not know when they might be moved. He also asserted to Foster that they were not brought to the city to be placed under fire. Jones concluded by reminding Foster that the only reason the prisoners had to be placed in Charleston was due to the refusal of the Federal government to exchange prisoners, a well-established policy recognized under the rules of civilized warfare.

In the first week of September, Jones did send to the Union lines a large number of Union surgeons and chaplains held as prisoners. They were returned without exchange. Though the stated policy was to refuse to accept them, Foster did allow them to cross the lines.

On September 7, the *Crescent City* moved to Lighthouse Inlet at the south end of Morris Island, where the six hundred Confederate officers disembarked. They were marched three miles along the beach to a stockade constructed for them between Fort Putnam (formerly Battery Gregg) and Fort Strong (formerly Battery Wagner).

They were guarded by the Fifty-fourth Massachusetts Volunteer Infantry (colored), commanded by Colonel Edward Hallowell. Hallowell became commanding officer after the fall of Colonel Robert Shaw in the July 18 assault on Battery Wagner. In that same battle, Hallowell was wounded in the groin and eye. He would prove to be a vicious warden at the prison.

One of the prisoners, Captain Thomas Pinckney, Fourth South Carolina Cavalry, wrote of his fellow prisoners:

> *A more disappointed and crestfallen set of men I have never seen, and none of us believed the United States Government was actually going to put its inhumane threat into execution, or how shells from our batteries falling*

short of Wagner or overshooting Gregg and bursting among our men would help the U.S. Government we failed to see.

The prisoners were marched into a stockade on a one-and-a-half-acre sand dune and assigned four men to a tent. Once in place, they were instructed as to the rules of the Morris Island prison. They were not allowed to gather in groups of more than ten men, though that was difficult to obey given that six hundred men were confined on a one-and-a-half-acre site. The prisoners were not allowed to build a fire. The entire prison was illuminated at night by calcium lights. The guards kept a Billinghurst-Requa machine gun, capable of firing 175 rounds per minute, trained on the camp.

Roll call was held every day at 6:30 a.m., noon and at retreat at the end of the day. After morning roll call, the prisoners would police the camp, rake the sand smooth and empty the latrines. Meals were served at 8:00 a.m. and 2:00 p.m. Taps was at 9:00 p.m., and every prisoner had to remain in his tent until morning roll call.

In September, the South Carolina heat was still tortuous in the day, particularly on a sand island with no trees or structures to provide shade.

The stockade on Morris Island that held the Confederate prisoners, known as the "Immortal 600," captive. *Courtesy of the Library of Congress.*

128

Additionally, the gnats and mosquitoes were a constant annoyance for which there was no relief.

The prisoners were shocked and infuriated to be intentionally placed in the line of fire. Lieutenant William Morgan, Eleventh Virginia Infantry, wrote of their situation, "We deplore the fact that the year of Our Lord 1864 has witnessed a scene so shocking to civilization and enlightenment, as hostages, and if need by martyrs, for our oppressed and struggling country's sake."

The prisoners were under fire from four sides with Forts Sumter and Moultrie to the north, Wagner to the south, the James Island batteries to the west and the fire from the monitors and Union fleet to the east. Foster had received word that the Union prisoners in Charleston were considering an escape, After September 7, he increased his rate of fire on the Confederate batteries and Charleston, hoping to distract the enemy and aid any escape.

Captain Morgan wrote of life in the camp:

> *What shelling was done was mostly done at night. Some of the shells burst over the stockade and the pieces would fall around, but I don't remember that any of the prisoners were hit. It was rather uncomfortable, though, to lie there and watch the big shells sailing through the air, which we could see at night by the fuse burning, and sometimes burst above us, instead of bursting in or above the Yankee forts 100 yards further on.*

The Union prisoners in Charleston were allowed three-quarters pound of fresh meat or one-half pound of salt meat, one-fifth pint of rice, one-half pound of hard bread and one-fifth pint of beans per day for their rations. While not luxurious rations, they were often more than noncombatants in Charleston lived on.

The Confederate prisoners on Morris Island were fed what the guards called "retaliation rations." Though Foster instructed Hallowell to feed the prisoners the same rations fed to Union troops in Charleston, Andersonville and Salisbury, Hallowell used the withholding of food to break down morale. Foster was issuing the rations, but Hallowell withheld them.

Lieutenant William W. Grace, Twenty-sixth Virginia Infantry, wrote about the rations served to the Confederate officers on Morris Island:

> *For rations we were furnished with three army crackers per day and a half pint of soup. The crackers were issued in the morning…About noon the half pint of soup was passed. It was called bean soup, but we could never discover any traces of that vegetable in the mixture.*

Captain George W. Nelson, Hanover (Virginia) Artillery, wrote of the worms that infested the crackers. He said, "Several persons, who, attempting to pick them out, having thrown out from fifty to eighty, stopped picking them out, not because the worms were all gone, but because the little bit of mush was going with them." On some days, they were issued a tablespoon of rice or two ounces of bacon.

After three weeks on Morris Island, rations were reduced one-quarter by Hallowell. Intestinal disorders became commonplace in the prison, and if not sick, the prisoners became weakened by the lack of properly sized rations.

They also suffered from a shortage of fresh water. Their water was obtained by digging shallow holes in the sand at their tents, hoping that enough fresh water would seep in. Frequently, holes dug too deep unearthed bodies buried in the sand during the Morris Island campaign. One Confederate officer wrote that the water was always "full of wiggle-tails."

On September 22, the prisoners were ordered to pack up and prepare to move. They were elated, thinking that their ordeal on Morris Island was over. They were organized into columns and marched down the beach to two schooners docked at Lighthouse Inlet.

The prisoners were divided into two groups and placed on the ships. Lieutenant James Ford, Twentieth Virginia Cavalry, noted that 275 prisoners were placed in the hold of the ship "filled with dirt and rubbish and abounding in rats of huge dimensions." Rumors spread through the ships that they were about to be exchanged and released to Charleston. Their hopes soon faded to disappointment when they were returned to the prison camp the next day.

As they marched up the beach, Captain James R. McMichael, Twelfth Georgia Infantry, expressed, "I looked around and every man was silent, head down. I wondered if any crowd marching to the grave of an esteemed friend could have so solemn and doleful an appearance." They were only moved to the schooners while guards searched the tents for any contraband or signs of an escape attempt.

Jones, frustrated with Foster's retaliation, threatened to place six hundred Union prisoners on the crumbled walls of Fort Sumter, though he never followed through. On September 16, Foster did allow mail and sutler privileges for the Confederate prisoners. This was the first mail allowed them since their arrival. Captain Henry Dickinson, Second Virginia Cavalry, wrote that during one sutler's visit he purchased ginger cakes and traded for beer made of potato peeling and sour molasses, a welcomed relief from "retaliation rations."

Predictably, the rough conditions, rancid water and poor rations were taking their toll. On September 27, Lieutenant William Callahan, Twenty-fifth Tennessee Cavalry, died of chronic diarrhea. This was followed by two additional deaths within the week.

In Charleston, a steamer, the *General Whiting*, arrived from Nassau, where the population was suffering from a yellow fever outbreak, and slipped through the blockade. Though the crew was quarantined, by mid-September a yellow fever epidemic befell Charleston. Jones notified Richmond that the fever had not yet spread to his Union prisoners, but they needed to be moved out of the city.

By October 8, all of the Union prisoners in Charleston had been transferred to either Florence or Columbia. On October 13, Jones notified Foster that he no longer held any Union prisoners in the city and asked that he remove the Confederate officers from Morris Island. Foster did not respond to the letter.

In mid-October, Foster allowed the Ladies' Aid Society of Charleston to send care boxes to the Confederate prisoners. The boxes contained tobacco, sweet potatoes and peanuts. Though the guards stole much of the rations, some were distributed to the prisoners. Captain David C. Grayson, Tenth Virginia Infantry, expressed, "Truly did it make each heart swell with pride, not so much for the article, but to know and feel that there is patriotism in the old land yet, and that we are still thought of by our countrymen, especially the women, God bless them!"

Though Foster never answered Jones, by late October 1864, he had transferred the Confederate prisoners from Morris Island to Fort Pulaski, Georgia, ending the retaliation ordeal.

13

"A Terrible, Heart-Breaking, Awful Night"

When General William T. Sherman marched out of Atlanta in November 1864, leaving a path of destruction and devastation behind him, his next destination was the subject of great speculation by the Confederate command. Troops and resources were pulled from Charleston and elsewhere in South Carolina to face him. The Fifth Georgia was moved from Charleston and sent to Macon, Georgia, to reinforce General Howell Cobb. Brigadier General James Chesnut Jr. also moved his South Carolina Reserves to Georgia. Confederate general William J. Hardee, headquartered in Charleston, also moved to Georgia, and Major General Robert Ransom arrived in Charleston to replace him. Soon, it was determined that Sherman was marching to Savannah.

On November 30, 1864, Union brigadier general Edward Hatch, commanding five thousand army troops and a naval brigade of five hundred sailors and marines, landed at Boyd's Neck, on the Broad River, just above Beaufort, South Carolina. He moved toward Grahamville with the objective to sever the Charleston and Savannah Railroad.

Confederate colonel Charles Colcock readied to meet Hatch but had few troops. Hardee sent General Gustavus W. Smith with two brigades of Georgia militia to reinforce Colcock. The combined Confederate forces confronted Hatch at Honey Hill, South Carolina, on November 30. During the battle, the Confederate forces were reinforced by the Forty-seventh Georgia, commanded by General Beverly H. Robertson, although the total Confederate troops engaged were no more than 1,400. In the daylong battle, Hatch could not dislodge the Confederates from their position, even though the

Union troops outnumbered the Confederates more than three to one. After nightfall, the Union troops withdrew to their transports at Boyd's Neck. Total Union casualties were 764, compared to only 47 for the Confederates.

During the six weeks of Sherman's March to the Sea in Georgia, little happened in Charleston. Union general Edward Hatch, now on Morris Island, observed, "The battering of Sumter is, in my opinion, an idle waste of material." General Halleck, in Washington, sent a dispatch to General Foster that General Grant "wanted the expenditure of ammunition upon Charleston and Fort Sumter discontinued."

Confederate general William J. Hardee. *Courtesy of the Library of Congress.*

South Carolina governor Milledge L. Bonham corresponded with Davis, asking him to reinforce the troops facing Sherman with troops from Virginia. General Robert E. Lee asserted, in a letter to Davis, "that if troops were removed from his command, and sent south it will necessitate the abandonment of Richmond."

In December, with Sherman close to Savannah, General Cooper wired Beauregard that he "hoped Savannah may be successfully defended, but the defense should not be too protracted to the sacrifice of the garrison. The same remark is applicable to Charleston."

Hardee evacuated Savannah on December 21, 1864. Upon occupying the city the next day, Sherman telegrammed Lincoln, "I beg to present you, as a Christmas gift, the City of Savannah, with 150 heavy guns and plenty of ammunition, and also about 25,000 bales of cotton."

While in Savannah, Sherman received a letter from General Halleck in Washington. Halleck stated:

An interior view of Fort Sumter in 1865. *Courtesy of the Library of Congress.*

Should you capture Charleston, I hope that by some accident the place may be destroyed, and if a little salt should be sown upon its site it may prevent the growth of future crops of nullification and secession.

Having already decided to march on Columbia, Sherman replied:

I will bear in mind your hint as to Charleston and don't think salt will be necessary. When I move, the Fifteenth Corps will be on the right of the Right Wing, and their position will bring them naturally, into Charleston first; and if you have watched the history of that corps you will have remarked that they generally do their work up pretty well. The truth is the whole army is burning with insatiable desire to wreck vengeance upon South Carolina. I almost tremble at her fate.

Sherman communicated to Foster in Hilton Head, "I regard any attempt to enter Charleston Harbor by its direct channel or to carry it by storm of James Island as too hazardous to warrant the attempt." However, Foster and Dahlgren made a show of force periodically to occupy the Confederate forces in Charleston, prohibiting their withdrawal to reinforce any attempt to slow or stop Sherman's movements.

"A Terrible, Heart-Breaking, Awful Night"

On the evening of January 15, 1865, Dahlgren dispatched the monitor *Patapsco* on patrol to look for harbor obstructions. While still eight hundred yards from Fort Sumter, it hit a mine and immediately sank. Sixty-two of the 105-man crew went down with the ship.

On January 30, 1865, Gillmore was ordered back to South Carolina to relieve Foster as commander of the Department of the South. Dahlgren was not pleased to see his old army colleague return. He recorded in his diary:

> *I have an entire contempt for Gillmore because of his conduct last year... So I briefly wrote to the Department stating that with his arrival to take command, asking to be relieved...I shall lose some prize money, too, but I will keep my self-respect which is better.*

In February, Fort Sumter still had a garrison of three hundred men from the Thirty-second Georgia Volunteers and two companies of the First South Carolina Artillery. The fort, though, was still nothing more than an infantry outpost except for the three guns on the northeast face guarding the shipping channel.

The interior of Fort Sumter after an intense bombardment and siege lasting 567 days, during which the Union army and navy fired a total of 46,053 artillery rounds on the fort. *Courtesy of the Collection of the U.S. House of Representatives.*

Leslie's war correspondent W.L. Crane sketched this Union assault on rifle pits held by the Palmetto Battalion on February 9, 1865. Confederate major Edward Manigault was wounded and taken prisoner in the attack. *Author's collection.*

On February 14, Beauregard sent instructions to evacuate Charleston. The Confederate troops were to travel by railroad through St. Stephens to Columbia and go to reinforce General Joseph E. Johnston in North Carolina. Union signalmen on Morris Island were intercepting messages from Charleston to the harbor forts regarding the pending evacuation.

On February 16, Major Thomas A. Huguenin, Confederate commander at Fort Sumter, received a telegraphic dispatch ordering that he prepare to evacuate his position. The next morning, a new Confederate flag was raised over Fort Sumter. At sunset, the flag was lowered, and a salute was fired. Near 10:00 p.m., two steamers, commanded by Lieutenant Thomas L. Swinton, arrived at Fort Sumter to evacuate the garrison. The roll was called, and the troops marched to the two ships. Major Huguenin, the commander; Lieutenant E.J. White, the fort's engineer; and Lieutenant W.G. Ogier, adjutant of the post, went to the ramparts and relieved the evening's sentinels, sending them to the boats.

In 1863, Huguenin had been the last to depart Battery Wagner in its evacuation. On the night of February 17, 1865, he was now the last to leave Fort Sumter. He recorded his thoughts that night in his report:

> *After visiting every portion of the fort, with a heavy heart I reached the wharf, no one was left behind but many a heart clung to those sacred and*

The interior of Fort Sumter after the Confederate evacuation in 1865. *Courtesy of the Library of Congress.*

The interior of Fort Moultrie, seen here after the Confederate evacuation. *Courtesy of the Library of Congress.*

battle scared ramparts, I cannot describe my emotions. I felt as if every tie held dear to me was about to be severed; the pride and glory of Sumter was there, and now in the gloom of darkness we were to abandon her, for whom every one of us would have shed the last drop of his blood.

Lee Harby, a young woman in Charleston, wrote of the events in Charleston on the night of the seventeenth and the next morning:

It was a terrible, heart-breaking, awful night. The men who were garrisoning Sumter had come over in their small boats, bringing their flags. In the early morning of the 18th, they were gathered in the city on the wharf, and there they cast themselves down on the earth and wept aloud. Some prayed; some cursed; all said they would rather have died in the fort they had so long defended than have her ramparts desecrated by the invader's tread.

Overnight, the Confederate troops prepared to destroy the military assets that could not be taken with them as they traveled to North Carolina. A large Blakely gun at the corner of East Battery and South Battery Streets was blown up. The charge was so intense that parts of the large gun penetrated the roof of a house one hundred yards away and lodged in the attic. The bridge across the Ashley River was set on fire.

The volunteer members of the white fire companies had long been converted to militia, and they departed with the Confederate troops. Only the city ward engines, manned by free blacks and slaves, were left to fight the many fires breaking out across the city.

Early on the morning of the eighteenth, a large magazine was set fire and exploded, causing a boom heard throughout the harbor. Supplies and ammunition were blown up at the Northeastern Railroad Depot. At the Cooper River docks, the Confederate gunboats *Palmetto State*, *Chicora* and *Charleston* were all blown up. The CSS *Stono*, formerly the USS *Isaac P. Smith*, was destroyed by fire. Warehouses containing thirty thousand bushels of rice and more than two thousand bales of cotton were burned.

The next day, the *Charleston Daily Courier* described the explosions that destroyed the gunboats:

The explosions were terrific. Tremendous clouds of smoke went up forming beautiful wreaths. A full Palmetto tree, with it leaves and stems was noticed by many observers. As the last wreath of smoke disappeared the full form of the rattlesnake in the center was remarked by many as it gradually faded away.

"A Terrible, Heart-Breaking, Awful Night"

After 567 days, the Siege of Charleston, the longest siege of the Civil War, ended with the evacuation of the Confederate troops.

On the morning of the eighteenth, the USS *Canonicus* fired several shots at Fort Moultrie and received no return fire. Major John A. Hennessy, Fifty-second Pennsylvania Infantry, departed Cummings Point on a small boat and was the first to arrive at Fort Sumter. Hennessy and the boat crew scaled the parapet and raised their regimental flag over Fort Sumter, the first Federal flag to fly over the fort since April 14, 1861. Union ships excitedly raced to the harbor forts hoping to be the first to raise the United States flag over the abandoned fortification.

Colonel Bennett, in a boat with Hennessy and twenty-five troops, docked at the Atlantic Wharf, near the foot of Broad Street, at 10:00 a.m. As he entered the city, George W. Williams, a city alderman, approached carrying a note from Mayor Charles Macbeth, reading, "The military authorities of the Confederate States have evacuated the city. I have remained to enforce law and preserve order until you take such steps as you may think best."

Two companies of the Fifty-second Pennsylvania and men from the Third Rhode Island Artillery landed in Charleston and accompanied Bennett to the Citadel, where headquarters was established. Bennett instructed Union troops to assist in fighting the many fires burning in the city from the night before.

As Union troops entered the city of Charleston, they were accompanied by W.T. Crane, a war correspondent writing for *Frank Leslie's Illustrated News*. Crane wrote of his observations in Charleston:

> *The appearance baffles all description; scarcely a house remains intact; in some instances a dozen shell have entered the same building; its glass invariably shattered in almost every window; roofs are crushed and walls lean, crack, and gape at you as you silently and thoughtfully gaze upon them; grass is growing in the streets...Crows scream around the ruins; broken bricks, timbers and debris of all kind are heaped around...Look at it now, and we see the blight of the touch of secession's fingers.*

Dahlgren recorded his thoughts as he approached Charleston by ship, "We passed Sumter, then Wagner, and all of the familiar scenery of the last two years; and so ends a command of two years of one of the largest fleets ever assembled under American Colors." After reaching the city, Dahlgren wired Welles, "Charleston has been abandoned by the rebels."

The ruins of the Circular Congregational Church in Charleston, burned in the fire of 1861. *Courtesy of the Library of Congress.*

An 1865 view of the ruins on Meeting Street in Charleston. *Courtesy of the Library of Congress.*

The ruins of St. John and St. Finbar Catholic Church on Broad Street in Charleston. *Courtesy of the Library of Congress.*

Though the ironclads were destroyed, seven of the "*Davids*" were discovered at Charleston. Dahlgren reported that another two of the torpedo steamers were recovered in the Cooper River, apparently scuttled by the Confederates.

A correspondent, identified as Berwick, with the *New York Tribune* also traveled to the city with Union troops. He described the wharves and city as he landed:

> *The wharves look as if they had been deserted for half a century—broken down, dilapidated, grass and moss peeping up between the pavement, where once the busy feet of commerce trod incessantly. The warehouses near the river; the streets as we enter them; the houses and the stores and the public buildings—we look at them and hold our breaths in utter amazement. Every step we take increases our astonishment. No pen, no pencil, no tongue can do justice to the scene…And, all around this area of desolation are the ruined houses that still stand—"Gillmore's Town" as the negroes call it.*

As Union troops found their way to Broad Street, they found the offices of the great secessionist newspaper, the *Mercury*, occupied by a black family.

The Post Office (Old Exchange Building) in Charleston in 1865. *Courtesy of the Library of Congress.*

The clubhouse of the Washington Racecourse in Charleston, site of a Federal prison camp. *Courtesy of the Library of Congress.*

On the western side of the city a great tragedy occurred when several young boys were playing around a burning cotton fire. They were taking handfuls of gunpowder from a nearby magazine and tossing them on the fire, amused as it ignited and sparked. Unknowingly, they left a trail of gunpowder from the fire to the gunpowder stores. Eventually, the powder ignited and followed the trail to the magazine, causing an enormous explosion that killed 150 people and burned and injured 200 others. Berwick reported, "The miserable victims were seen tumbling about in agony, literally roasting alive; their wild shrieks were appalling—and all help was impossible."

The 127th New York Volunteers and the 21st United States Colored Troops (USCT) were established as the garrison to occupy Charleston. They were commanded by General Schimmelfennig. He

In this *Harper's Weekly* engraving, Lieutenant Colonel Augustus Bennett leads the Fifty-fifth Massachusetts Volunteer Infantry (colored) through the streets of Charleston on February 21, 1865. *Author's collection.*

established his headquarters at the Miles Brewton House at 27 King Street. Interestingly, the same house was occupied to serve as British headquarters in 1780 after the fall of the city.

By Sunday, February 19, soldiers from the 21st USCT and others were wildly cavorting through Charleston looting all the homes, businesses and public buildings. Colonel W.H. Davis, 104th Pennsylvania, wrote of the looting:

> *The plunder was not obtained by all soldiers, but officers received a share. Their conduct in this particular was disgraceful, and should have cost the offending ones their commission. Some of them sent north pianos, elegant furniture, silverware, books, pictures, etc. to adorn their New England dwellings.*

In March 1865, Secretary of War Edwin M. Stanton, on behalf of President Lincoln, issued the following order:

> *At the hour of noon, on the 14th day of April, 1865, Brevet Major-General Anderson will raise and plant upon the ruins of Fort Sumter, in Charleston harbor, the same United States flag which floated over the battlements of that fort during the rebel assault, and which was lowered and saluted by*

Brevet Major General John P. Hatch and his staff at his headquarters established in the city after the fall of Charleston. *Courtesy of the Library of Congress.*

This *Frank Leslie's* engraving depicts Union gunboats clearing Charleston Harbor of mines, torpedoes and iron and pine boom obstructions after the fall of Charleston in February 1865. *Author's collection.*

After placing Charleston under martial law, Union brigadier general Alexander Schimmelfennig required citizens to take an oath of allegiance to the United States. *Author's collection.*

Rations of rice, cornmeal and salt were distributed to starving Charlestonians at West Point Mill on the Ashley River, as depicted on this engraving published in *Frank Leslie's Illustrated News*. *Author's collection.*

him, and the small force of his command, when the works were evacuated on the 14th of April, 1861.

On the morning of April 14, a crowd of more than five thousand people booked passage to Fort Sumter. The wharf at the fort was lined with a

The Federal squadron assembled off Fort Sumter on April 14, 1865. *Courtesy of the Library of Congress.*

company of soldiers "with muskets shouldered and bayonets fixed—on the left, white, on the right, black, rivaling each other in soldierly bearing."

Wooden steps had to be constructed over the wall of Fort Sumter to allow entrance. Abner Doubleday, Norman Hall and Peter Hart, all men who served at Fort Sumter with Robert Anderson, were in attendance.

As Robert Anderson stepped to the flagstaff, he was met by Peter Hart, who, from a mailbag, retrieved the flag that was removed from Fort Sumter on April 14, 1861, for all to see—to the roars of the crowd. Anderson was overwhelmed by the moment and could not raise the flag alone. With the help of Hart and several sailors there, the Fort Sumter flag was raised to the top of the 150-foot-tall flagstaff as the band played "The Star-Spangled Banner" and the crowd wept and hugged. A one-hundred-gun salute was fired from Fort Sumter, followed by gun salutes fired from the former Confederate batteries surrounding the harbor.

At 6:00 p.m., a grand dinner was given by General Hatch in Charleston. The evening was filled with many speeches and toasts. The final toast of the evening was reserved for Robert Anderson. After his introductory remarks, he raised his glass and offered:

Guests and officials await the ceremonies at Fort Sumter on April 14, 1865. *Courtesy of the Library of Congress.*

I beg you now, that you will join me in drinking to the health of another man whom we all love to honor, the man who, when elected President of the United States, was compelled to reach the seat of government with an escort, but now could travel all over the country with millions of hands and hearts to sustain him. I give you the good, the great, the honest man, Abraham Lincoln.

The many people enjoying the gala evening, of course, did not know that as they toasted Lincoln, John Wilkes Booth would fire the fateful shot at the president's head at Ford's Theatre in Washington.

In May, General William T. Sherman visited Charleston and appropriately suggested, "Anyone who is not satisfied with war should go and see Charleston, and he will pray louder and deeper than ever that the country may in the future be spared any more war."

BIBLIOGRAPHY

Bostick, Douglas W. *The Confederacy's Secret Weapon: Frank Vizetelly and the Illustrated London News.* Charleston, SC: The History Press, 2009.

———. *Secession to Siege: The Charleston Engravings.* Charleston, SC: Joggling Board Press, 2004.

———. *The Union Is Dissolved! Charleston and Fort Sumter in the Civil War.* Charleston, SC: The History Press, 2009.

Brennan, Patrick. *Secessionville: Assault on Charleston.* N.p.: Savas Publishing Company, 1996.

Browning, Robert M., Jr. *Success Is All that Was Expected: The South Atlantic Blockading Squadron during the Civil War.* Washington, D.C.: Brassey's Inc., 2002.

Burton, E. Milby. *The Siege of Charleston: 1861–1865.* Columbia: University of South Carolina Press, 1970.

Charleston Daily Courier, 1861–65.

Charleston Mercury, 1861–65.

———. "Special Orders # 62." May 2, 1863.

Coker, P.C., III. *Charleston's Maritime Heritage, 1670–1865,* Charleston, SC: CokerCraft Press, 1987.

Dahlgren, Madeline Vinton. *Memoir of John A. Dahlgren, Rear-Admiral of the United States Navy.* Boston, 1882.

Floyd, Viola Caston, comp. "The Fall of Charleston." *South Carolina Historical Magazine* 66 (January 1965): 1–7.

Frank Leslie's Illustrated Newspaper, 1861–65.

Fraser, Walter J., Jr. *Charleston! Charleston!: The History of a Southern City.* Columbia: University of South Carolina Press, 1989.

French, Justus Clement, and Edward Cary. *The Trip of the Steamer* Oceanus *to Fort Sumter and Charleston, S.C. Comprising the Programme of Exercises at the Re-Raising of the Flag over the Ruins of Fort Sumter, April 14th, 1865.* Brooklyn: The Union Steam Printing House, 1865.

Fuzzleburg, Fritz (alias). *Prison Life During the Rebellion: The Miseries and Sufferings of Six Hundred Confederate Prisoners Sent from Fort Delaware to Morris Island to be Punished.* Singer's Glen, VA: Joseph Funk's Sons, Printers, 1869.

Gilchrist, Major Robert. *The Confederate Defense of Morris Island, Charleston Harbor.* Charleston, SC: New and Courier Book Presses, 1887.

Gilmore, Q.A. *Engineer and Artillery Operations Against the Defenses of Charleston Harbor.* New York, 1865.

———. *Supplementary Engineer and Artillery Operations Against the Defenses of Charleston Harbor.* New York, 1868.

Hagood, Johnson. *Memoirs of the War of Secession.* Columbia, SC: The State Company, 1910.

Harper's Weekly Journal of Civilization, 1861–65.

"Honour Letters." Unpublished, n.d.

Hoole, William Stanley. *Vizetelly Covers the Confederacy.* Tuscaloosa: University of Alabama Press, 1957.

Illustrated London News, 1861–65.

Johnson, John. *The Defense of Charleston Harbor Including Fort Sumter and the Adjacent Sea Islands, 1863–1865.* Charleston, SC: Walker, Evans, and Cogswell, 1890.

Jones, Samuel. *The Siege of Charleston and the Operations on the South Atlantic Coast in the War Among the States.* New York: The Neale Publishing Company, 1911.

Joslyn, Mauriel P. *Immortal Captives: The Story of 600 Confederate Officers and the United States Prisoner of War Policy.* Gretna, LA: Pelican Publishing Company, 2008.

Minutes of the Washington Light Infantry. Charleston, SC.

Orvin, Maxwell Clayton. *In South Carolina Waters, 1861–1865.* Charleston, SC: Nelsons' Southern Printing & Publishing Company, 1961.

Parker, William H. *Recollections of a Naval Officer, 1841–1865.* Annapolis, MD: Naval Institute Press, 1985.

Roman, Alfred. *The Military Operations of General Beauregard in the War Between the States, 1861 to 1865.* New York: Harper and Brothers, 1883.

Schreadley, R.L. *Valor and Virtue: The Washington Light Infantry in Peace and In War.* Spartanburg, SC: The Reprint Publishers, 1997.

Southern Historical Collection. James H. Tomb Papers. University of North Carolina at Chapel Hill.

"Stories of a Confederate." *National Magazine* 10 (April 1899–September 1899): 41–54.

War of the Rebellion: A Compilation of the Official Records of the Union and Confederate Armies. Washington, D.C.: U.S. Government Printing Office, 1880–1901.

War of the Rebellion: A Compilation of the Official Records of the Union and Confederate Navies. Washington, D.C.: U.S. Government Printing Office, 1894–1922.

Wilcox, Arthur M., and Warren Ripley. *The Civil War at Charleston.* Charleston, SC: The Evening Post Publishing Company, 1966.

Wise, Stephen R. *Gate of Hell: Campaign for Charleston Harbor, 1863.* Columbia: University of South Carolina Press, 1994.

INDEX

A

Alabama, CSS 41
American Diver, USS 113
Ammen, Daniel 59
Anderson, Robert 9, 74, 118, 143, 146
Andersonville 123, 124, 129
Arkansas, CSS 41
Ashley River 23, 24, 138, 145
Atlanta Rolling Mill 44
Augusta, USS 15, 52, 54, 55
Austin, Charles, Jr. 49

B

Bache, Alexander 13
Banks, Nathaniel 116
Barnard, John G. 13
Barton 109
Battery Cheves 40, 51
Battery Glover 40
Battery Gregg 40, 69, 70, 75, 90, 93–96, 98, 102, 103, 127, 128
Battery Island 27, 33
Battery Marshall 115
Battery Pringle 51, 118
Battery Tynes 51
Battery Wagner 40, 57, 68–78, 80, 81, 83, 84, 90, 93–98, 102, 104, 127–129, 136, 139
Battery Wampler 40
Bay Point 13, 18
Beauregard, P.G.T. 13, 18, 31, 39–41, 45, 47, 48, 50, 55, 58, 66, 69, 71, 72, 78–82, 87, 89, 90, 92, 93, 95, 96, 98, 105–108, 110, 112, 115, 116, 118, 133, 136
Benham, Henry 34–38
Benjamin, Judah 19, 55
Bermuda 11
Bienville, USS 15, 52
Billinghurst-Requa machine gun 128
Black Island 92
Boate, Edward W. 124
Bonham, Milledge L. 133
Booth, John Wilkes 147
Boston Journal 80
Boutelle, Charles 21, 23
Boyd's Neck 132, 133
Bragg, Braxton 39, 78

Broad Street 106, 110, 116, 122, 123, 139, 141
Brown, J. Webman 49
Bull's Bay 13

C

Calhoun, E.B. 48
Calhoun Street 92, 113
Callahan, William 131
Cameron & Company 44, 109
Camp Lawton 124
Canandaigua, USS 58
Cannon, J. Walker 110, 111
Canonicus, USS 139
Carlin, James 109
Castle Pinckney 11, 23, 40
Catskill, USS 59, 61–63, 72, 73
Charleston and Savannah Railroad 23, 25, 72, 118, 132
Charleston Daily Courier 43, 45, 47, 73, 78, 113, 138
Charleston Mercury 22, 42, 44, 141
Chaulk, John 110
Chesapeake Bay 13
Chesnut, James, Jr. 132
Chesterfield, CSS 51
Cheves, Langdon 61
Chicheshee, Mrs. C.E. 23
Chicora, CSS 43–47, 51, 53, 54, 56, 66, 100, 101, 107, 108, 114, 138
Church Street 106, 116
Citadel, the 139
Cobb, Howell 132
Colcock, Charles 132
Coles Island 26–28, 30, 39
Columbus Street 43
Commodore McDonough, USS 49, 50
Concord Street 44
Conover, Lieutenant 48–50
Cooper River 29, 46, 109, 138, 141
Coosawatchie 23

C.P. Williams, USS 47
Crescent City, USS 126, 127
Cummings Point 105, 139
Curlew, USS 15

D

Daffodil, USS 100
Dahlgren gun 11, 47, 66, 67
Dahlgren, John A. 67, 72, 74, 82, 84, 93, 97, 98, 100, 101, 102, 112, 116, 118, 121, 134, 135, 139, 141
Dantzler, O.M. 115
David, CSS 110–112
Davis, Jefferson 25, 80
Dawhoo River 118
Dawn, USS 47
Dickinson, Henry 130
Dixon, George E. 115
Doubleday, Abner 146
Downes, John 59, 63
Drayton, Percival 16, 59, 61
Drayton, Thomas 16, 18, 19
Duke, Basil 123
Dunkle, John J. 126
Dunovant, R.G.M. 17, 19
Du Pont, Samuel Francis 13, 14, 15, 18, 20, 21, 26, 30, 41, 47, 54–59, 61, 65–68

E

Eason & Brothers 43
Eason, James M. 43, 46
East Battery 138
Easterby, Samuel 110
Eastport, CSS 41
Ebaugh, David C. 110
Echo 11
Ella and Annie 109
Elliott, Stephen 98, 101, 104, 105, 116
Elliott Street 116

Etiwan 51
Ettaone 29

F

Fairfax, D. McN. 59
Fickling, E.S. 109
Fishing Rip Shoal 15
Flag, USS 52
Flat Rock 28
Florida, CSS 41
Folly Island 68, 69, 72, 86, 102
Folly River 32, 82
Fort Beauregard 13, 17, 18, 40
Fort Delaware 126
Fortescue, Louis R. 125
Fort Monroe 11, 116
Fort Moultrie 30, 31, 40, 55, 61,
    64, 71, 101, 102, 129, 139
Fort Pulaski 131
Fort Putnam 102, 103, 127
Fort Ripley 40
Fort Strong 102, 104, 127
Fort Sumter 9, 11–13, 26, 29, 40,
    47, 51, 55, 57, 58, 59, 61–69,
    74, 75, 82, 83, 87, 90, 93,
    96, 98–105, 109, 112, 113,
    116–121, 129, 130, 133–139,
    143, 145, 146
Fort Walker 13, 15–18
Foster, John G. 57, 118, 121–123,
    126, 127, 129–131, 133–135
Fox, Gustavus 21, 57, 58
Frank Leslie's Illustrated News 37, 139

G

Gadsden Alley 116
Gaillard, Palmer C. 74
Gaillard, P.C. 35, 36
Gelzer, Mrs. Sue L. 43, 44, 45
Gem of the Sea, USS 14
General Clinch 51
General Parkhill 12

Gillmore, Quincy A. 26, 30, 57, 68,
    69, 71–74, 78–81, 83, 85, 86,
    87, 89–93, 96, 100, 101, 102,
    113, 116, 118, 135, 141
Gist, States Rights 30, 31
Glassel, William T. 108, 110, 111,
    112
Godon, Sylanus 16
Gosport Navy Yard 11, 42
Grace, William W. 129
Grimball Plantation 32, 33, 38,
    48–50

H

Hagood, Johnson 27, 33, 77, 105
Halleck, Henry W. 69, 92, 93, 126,
    133
Hall, Norman 146
Hallowell, Edward 75, 127, 129, 130
Harby, Lee 138
Harleston, F.H. 48
Harriet Lane, USS 12
Harris, D.B. 66
Hart, Peter 146
Hartstene, Henry J. 51
Hatch, Edward 132, 133
Hatch, John P. 118, 144, 146
Hatteras Inlet 13
Hayne, T.B. 48
Hennessy, John A. 139
Hibernian Hall 44
Higginson, Thomas W. 72
Hilton Head 13, 19, 25, 38, 41, 57,
    82, 122, 134
H.L. Hunley 114–115
Hog Island 40
Honey Hill 132
Honour, Theodore 104
Housatonic, USS 51, 52, 54, 58, 114,
    115
Huguenin, Thomas A. 96, 121,
    136

Hunley, Horace L. 113
Hunter, David 26, 30, 32, 34, 37, 38, 57, 68, 71
Huron, USS 58

I

Illustrated London News 58
Ingraham, Duncan 45, 51, 53, 55
Isaac P. Smith, USS 14, 15, 48, 51, 62, 112, 138

J

Jacksonborough 72
James Island 24, 26, 30–34, 38, 40, 41, 48–51, 69, 72, 75, 80, 81, 82, 85, 89, 93, 98, 105, 106, 118, 129, 134
Jefferson Davis 12
John Fraser & Company 12, 43, 45, 109
John's Island 30, 49, 50, 118
Johnson, John 82
Johnston, Joe 78, 81
Johnston, Joseph E. 136
Jones, Francis M. 43
Jones, Iredell 36
Jones, Samuel 116, 117, 122, 125–127, 130, 131

K

Keitt, L.M. 96
Keokuk, USS 58, 59, 62–67, 100
Keystone State, USS 52–55
Kiawah Island 102
King's Creek 118
Knight, Charles W. 74

L

LaCoste, Adolphus W. 66
Ladies' Aid Society of Charleston 131
Lady Davis, CSS 14

Lamar, Thomas G. 34–37
Leasure, Daniel 36
Lee, Francis D. 13, 107
Lee, Robert E. 19, 20, 23–26, 33, 81, 116, 133
Lehigh 104
Le Roy, William E. 53, 54
Lighthouse Creek 86
Lighthouse Inlet 68, 72, 127, 130
Lincoln, Abraham 9, 11, 30, 57, 67, 68, 69, 122, 124, 133, 143, 147
Live Yankee, USS 109
Louisiana, CSS 41

M

Macbeth, Charles 139
Maffit's Channel 22
Magnolia, USS 52
Mahone, William 11
Mallory, Stephen Russell 41, 42, 43, 107, 112
Manigault, Edward 116, 136
Marion Hospital 125
McClintock, James 113
McKethan, H. 74
Memphis, USS 52, 54, 55
Mercedita, USS 52–55
Mercury 15
Miles Brewton House 143
Miles, William Porcher 81
Mississippi, CSS 41
Mitchel, John C. 49, 116, 117, 121
Mohican, USS 15, 16
Montauk, USS 47, 59, 61, 72
Morgan, William 129
Morris Island 20, 40, 57, 58, 65, 68, 69, 71, 72, 73, 78, 80–87, 89, 93–97, 98–101, 102, 105, 112, 115, 118, 121, 122, 127–131, 133, 136
Moultrie House 41

N

Nahant, USS 59, 62, 63, 72
Nantucket, USS 59, 61, 62
Nassau 11, 52, 131
Nelson, George W. 130
New Ironsides, USS 47, 56, 58, 59, 61, 63–66, 74, 82, 93, 109–112, 116
New Town Creek 32
New York Herald 22, 67
New York Times 14, 22
New York Tribune 34, 141
Niagara, USS 11, 12
Northeastern Railroad Depot 138
North Edisto River 82, 112, 118

O

O'Connor, James 122
Ogier, W.G. 48, 136
Onward, USS 29
Osceola, USS 14
Ottawa, USS 14, 15, 30, 52, 112

P

Palmetto State, CSS 43–46, 51–56, 66, 107, 108, 114, 138
Passaic, USS 59–62, 82
Patrick Henry, CSS 45
Pawnee, USS 15, 100
Payne, John A. 114
Peerless, USS 14
Pemberton, John C. 25–27, 30–33, 39, 70, 81
Pembina, USS 14, 15, 30
Penguin, USS 14, 15
Pennsylvania, USS 45
Pickens, Francis D. 9, 13, 18, 23, 26, 27, 30, 39, 40, 107, 108
Pickering, Charles 115
Pinckney, Thomas 127
Pioneer 113

Planter 28–31
Porter, John 43, 44
Port Royal 13, 14, 16–19, 23, 30, 32, 34, 47, 48, 55, 58, 59, 65, 72, 109, 118, 127
Powhatan, USS 108
Princess Royal 51, 54, 114
Prison Oglethorpe 124
Pritchard Street 44
Putnam, Haldiman S. 74, 102

Q

Quaker City, USS 52, 54

R

Randolph, George W. 41
Ransom, Robert 132
Ravenel, Dr. St. Julien 109, 110
R.B. Forbes 15
Resolute, CSS 14
Rhett, Alfred 58, 59, 61, 66, 82, 98
Rhind, A.C. 59, 64
Ripley, Roswell 18, 19, 48, 58, 66
Robertson, Beverly H. 132
Rutledge, John 45, 51

S

Sampson, CSS 14
Sass, J.K. 107
Savannah, CSS 14
Schimmelfennig, Alexander 118, 142, 145
Schirmer, Jacob 92, 116
Secessionville 32, 36–39, 69, 74
Seddon, James A. 80, 81, 125, 126
Seminole, USS 12
Seneca, USS 14, 15, 47
Seward, William 23
Seymour, Thomas 74
Seymour, Truman 57, 68
Shaw, Robert 74, 75, 78, 127

Sherman, Thomas W. 13–15, 19, 26, 30
Sherman, William T. 132–135, 147
Slidell, John 55
Smalls, Robert 28 30
Sol Legare Island 33, 34
South Atlantic Blockading Squadron 13, 26, 48
South Battery 138
Southern Torpedo Company 109, 110, 112
Southern Wharf 28
Stanton, Edwin 143
Stettin, USS 52
Stevens, Isaac 34
Stevenson, T.G. 74, 76
St. Helena Sound 13
St. James Parish 116
St. Michael's 33, 86, 105
St. Michael's Alley 106
Stoney, Theodore D. 109, 110
Stono, CSS 138
Stono River 24, 26, 27, 30, 31–34, 41, 48, 49, 51, 62, 72, 118
St. Paul's 113
St. Philip's Church 56, 113
Stringham, Silas Horton 13
Strong, George 73–75, 78, 102
Sullivan's Island 20, 40, 41, 67, 80, 93, 105, 115
Susquehanna, USS 15, 16
Swamp Angel 86–88, 91, 92

T

Taliaferro, William B. 74
Tennessee, CSS 41
Terry, A.H. 72
Torch, CSS 108, 109
Tower Battery 32, 34–37
Tredegar Foundry 44
Trenholm, George S. 43

U

Unadilla, USS 15, 29, 30, 51, 52, 58
United States Colored Troops 142
U.S. Signal Corps 125

V

Vandalia, USS 12, 14, 15
Vattel, de Emmerich 71, 72
Virginia, CSS 41, 43, 61
Vixen, USS 14
Vizetelly, Frank 58, 61, 64, 77, 87–89, 91
Vogdes, I. 68

W

Wabash, USS 12, 15, 16, 47
Wagener, John A. 16
Wagner, Theodore D. 109
Wappoo Creek 24, 32, 41, 48, 51
Watson, Baxter 113
Welles, Gideon 12, 13, 20, 30, 41, 57, 58, 67, 139
West, Daniel 77
Whiting, W.H.C. 78
Winan, Ross 109
Wissahickon, USS 47, 58
Worden, John L. 59, 61, 62
Wright, Horatio G. 34, 38

Y

Yates, Joseph A. 48–51, 62, 118
Yeardon, Richard 45

About the Author

D oug Bostick is a native of James Island and is an eighth-generation South Carolinian. He is a graduate of the College of Charleston and earned a master's degree from the University of South Carolina. Bostick is a former staff and faculty member of the University of South Carolina and the University of Maryland.

He is the author of fifteen books, and his knowledge of history is enhanced by a raconteur's gift for storytelling. He speaks on a wide range of topics, including the history of the Sea Islands, South Carolina horse racing, the War Between the States, root work in South Carolina, Lowcountry folklore and the history of Lowcountry food.

Bostick is the chairman of the First Shot Commemorative Committee, organizing an event planned for April 12, 2011.

Visit us at
www.historypress.net